Russian Liberalism

FROM GENTRY TO INTELLIGENTSIA

George Fischer

HARVARD UNIVERSITY PRESS

Cambridge, Massachusetts

Distributed in Great Britain by Oxford University Press, London

FOR MY PARENTS

This volume was prepared under a grant from the
Carnegie Corporation of New York. That Corporation is not, however, the author, owner, publisher,
or proprietor of this publication and is not to be
understood as approving by virtue of its grant any
of the statements made or views expressed therein.

Library of Congress Catalog Card Number 57–13462
SBN 674-78180-5
Printed in the United States of America

FOREWORD

The longer I studied Russian liberalism, the more it fascinated me as an unexplored vantage point for much analyzed and central problems: Russian historical evolution, the nature of Russia's intelligentsia, the West's own liberalism, underdeveloped societies. This is the framework of my book.

The history of Russian liberalism stretches from the eighteenth century to the 1917 Revolution. Of this span, the present book covers only a middle portion — from the Great Reforms of the 1860's to the 1905 Revolution. It is in these four or five decades that Russian liberalism undergoes its major transformation, the transformation from gentry to intelligentsia — socially from the middling landowning nobility to the new professional middle class, politically from rural self-government (the zemstvo) to a mass party (the Kadets). This is the book's thesis.

The thesis grows in part out of the definition of liberalism itself. As a term, "liberalism" is generic rather than specific. The varieties of liberal experience may be defined jointly as the peculiarly Western individualism of the eighteenth, nineteenth, and twentieth centuries. The ends and means of this individualism have emphasized society rather than the individual himself: the ends a society in which the individual is central as well as self-governing; the means institutionalized liberties like private property and the supremacy of law. Beyond that, the varieties of liberal experience — universal or particular ideas, movements, and institutions — differ with each time and each place. Within this general definition of liberalism, a further distinction is desirable. It is the distinction between "have-not" liberalism and liberals of advanced countries. Have-not liberalism is a minority movement in an underdeveloped society. Here it cannot espouse the same attitudes or tactics as in the few wholly liberal societies on the northern shores of the Atlantic. This remains true no matter how similar the symbols: terminology, program, ideology. Equally basic is yet another distinction, the distinction between the have-not liberals who seek their goals through the existing illiberal government and those whose hopes lie in its overthrow or drastic transformation. This particular distinction has long caused bitterness, or at least confusion, among participants and observers alike. Almost invariably, the term "liberal" is claimed for one type and denied to the other.

My thesis is shaped as well by the historical context of have-not liberalism: an underdeveloped society. Currently the term "underdeveloped society" stands almost exclusively for economic development on the one hand and on the other for the ex-colonial areas of Asia and Africa acquiring statehood after World War II. Such usage is too narrow. Already in post-medieval Europe variations occurred in the shift from "underdeveloped" to "modern" — to ever spreading and ever more complex organization of men, of ideas, of tools. The continent lagged behind Britain; even quite recent events in France and Germany, not to mention Southern and Eastern Europe, can best be understood as functions of underdevelopment. And in Europe, as elsewhere, underdevelopment was as much cultural, political, and psychological as economic. Russia, too, was an underdeveloped society until its second industrial revolution of the 1930's, and it continues to share as many characteristics with the newest states of Asia and Africa as with the "modern" (and liberal) societies bunched around one portion of the Atlantic Ocean.

Hence when we speak of Russian liberals, the reader's

analogy should never be with the familiar images of nine-teenth-century Germany or England or the United States. Farfetched though it may seem at first glance, a more valid analogy is with the Spain and Greece of the 1820's — or present-day Asia and Latin America. And of the two different types of have-not liberals, in Russia both are in evidence during the period treated in this book. I have paid a good deal more attention to one type — the more militant — than to the other. I have done this not because I preferred one or was unaware of the other. I have done it because, in the half century between the Great Reforms and the 1905 Revolution, it is these militants within Russian liberalism who were on the rise, who came to influence Russia's history more and more. This was not so before or after, and it may not have been "a Good Thing." That it was so then is the thesis of my book.

Technically, this book has tried to combine the monograph's complete documentation with the advantages of an essay: brevity and less inhibited generalizations. Since the subject has not been explored systematically, the alternative would have been a massive compendium too detailed for all but the specialists. For these, the "end notes" contain abbreviated citations of primary data. As a rule, the full title of each work cited appears in the bibliography at the end of the text, together with a discussion of the principal sources relied upon and a list of acknowledgments. To those listed, and to all others who helped, my warmest thanks.

George Fischer

CONTENTS

ILLUSTRATIONS

Following page 226

Russian Liberalism

Chapter One

SMALL DEEDS OR
SENSELESS DREAMS?

Although this aspiration to bring his ideals from the empyrean to the field of actuality did smack of something politically dangerous, the Liberal glowed with such sincerity of zeal, and moreover was such a dear and so nice to everyone, that he was forgiven even for being politically unsound. He knew how to vindicate truth with a smile, could, when necessary, play the simpleton, and could show off his disinterestedness to advantage. But chiefly he never demanded anything at the point of the sword, but always only within the limits of possibility.

Saltykov-Shchedrin, *Fables*

A century ago, liberalism was growing in all of the newly modernizing "have-not" nation-states, from Central Europe to East Asia. But beneath were layer upon layer of premodern social tissue that resisted the scope and pace of modernization. In such an environment, liberalism could rarely begin to approximate the slow, sturdy liberal growth on the northern shores of the Atlantic. Instead, in other underdeveloped societies as much as in Russia, a have-not liberalism as a rule oscillated between the prosaic compromises of "small deeds" and the opposite extreme of "senseless dreams."

In the mid-1890's Russia's new and last tsar dramatically charged some liberal noblemen with harboring "senseless dreams." By then the accusation was not unjustified, although it took another decade before these senseless dreams were really voiced. During the 1860's–1890's, "senseless dreams" had served only as a hazy leitmotiv, and a different Russian term — namely "small deeds" — characterized the activities of these earlier liberals. It was not until the 1880's that this term gained currency among dispirited Russian socialists. But to the liberals it may be applied two decades earlier, from the time when Alexander II's Great Reforms lost momentum in the early 1860's.

I

A vast gulf divides the politics of the liberal Occident from Russian politics before the 1905 Revolution. For politics as we know it hardly existed in Russia at all, if politics means the attempt "to influence the distribution of power," and power in turn refers to a state "that (successfully) claims the monopoly of the legitimate use of physical force within a given territory" (to follow Max Weber's "Politics as a Vocation"). In Russia a traditional autocracy monopolized not only power but politics as well. Specifically, there were no elective national legislature or political parties, the institutionalized Western form of politics. The absence of political parties also precluded their Western appurtenances: the organized machine or caucus, the professional politician, the electoral victor's spoils of offices and honors, the charismatic mass leader.

If the state monopolizes not only power but also the means by which power is affected, and if no legislature or political parties exist, can there be any politics at all outside the state? In Russia and the other major autocracies like Prussia, Austria-Hungary, and Japan, such politics did emerge, but with a unique set of actors and arenas. The actors were most often individual "notables," independently wealthy men to whom politics was an avocation only. And the absence of legal and formalized channels for politics outside the state forced such politically minded notables to seek other, formally nonpolitical arenas. Often the press became one such arena; according to Weber, "Only the journalist is a paid professional; only the management of the newspaper is a continuous political organization." Russia's liberal notables after the Great Reforms confirmed the importance of the press. Their activities, their thinking, their mood had been voiced (and shaped) particularly by Korsh's S. *Peterburgskie vedomosti* until the mid-1870's and after that by the "professorial" Moscow *Russkie vedomosti,* and among the journals by Stasiulevich's *Vestnik Evropy* in St. Petersburg and to a lesser extent by Goltsev's *Russkaia mysl* in Moscow.

Not only, however, did Russian autocracy tolerate the press as a substitute for institutionalized politics outside the state, but during the Great Reforms of the 1860's the autocracy itself created the outstanding new arena: local self-government. In this arena Russian liberalism focused its politics after the Great Reforms, and here the "small deeds" liberal notables were most active between the 1860's and the 1890's.

Both before and after the Great Reforms, these liberal notables — the independently wealthy dilletanti in politics — emanated from the nobility. But there was a difference. In the earlier period, the liberals stressed emancipation of the serfs. This isolated them from their own class and meant that liberalism then was confined to individual writing and theorizing. The only larger ventures were Nikolai Novikov's short-lived Enlightenment campaign through Freemasonry, at the end of the eighteenth century, and the still briefer semiliberal conspiracy of the Decembrists. Only after the Great Reforms did the liberals operate not against the nobility but within one of its segments, the gentry.*

* Technically, the term "gentry" is synonymous with "nobility," that is, a landowning class with some hereditary privilege. But in Russia, as elsewhere in Europe, the nobility tended to divide into two parts according to origin and to function. With respect to origin, a more ancient nobility, once sovereign and hence aristocratic, was in early modern times augmented by a service nobility created by the rising monarchs. In terms of function, the service nobility inclined toward military service, local administration, and smaller landowning, while the aristocracy oscillated between high

It was no mere accident that after the Great Reforms the gentry was for many years the major source of Russian liberalism. Education, worldliness, and access to the state made the nobility the only class in nineteenth-century Russia that dared engage in politics. The one other potential source of independently wealthy notables, the business "bourgeoisie," did not. Neither did the aristocratic segment of the nobility, since large estates and in particular high government offices bound it more tightly to the state and the *status quo*. The gentry had the aristocracy's qualifications for leadership without most of its economic and career advantages.

Furthermore, the gentry never quite adjusted economically to the revolution in Russian agriculture caused by the freeing of serfs in the Emancipation of 1861. Large-scale capitalist farming, then becoming fashionable in Russia, was beyond its means — and clashed with its anti-business traditions, which were reminiscent of the French nobility. The world agricultural crisis of the 1870's, which in Russia lingered on until the end of the century, made matters still worse. A last blow came in the 1890's, when the favoritism of industry became official state policy. As a result, the whole of the nobility lost its landholdings at a disastrous rate, one third of them in the last three decades of the nineteenth century and half by 1905.

A mood of despondency resulted, and a hearty dislike for the government's professional administrators, the "bureaucracy," which was blamed most often for the nobility's and the country's ailments. It would be wrong, however, to conclude that the Russian gentry was therefore ripe for

office in the central state and their own large estates. As a result, in common parlance, and in this study as well, "gentry" refers to the new lesser squirearchy, and "aristocracy" to the numerically slight older and higher nobility.

political opposition. For the gentry, like the whole nobility, was a class that a strong state had pampered for centuries with economic advantages, social privileges, government offices. This age-long process, accompanied by increased political impotence and dependence on the state, made a *Fronde* far less likely than its opposite. In common with the Russian aristocracy, the gentry preferred continued patronage to political action outside the state, against the state.

Yet the economic crisis was unmistakable; the officials' ascendancy offended the nobility's rarely asserted claims to elite status; there was fear of revolution from below and of favoritism of industry from above. Thus a subtle change did take place after the Great Reforms in this economically insolvent, politically impotent, but socially and financially still pampered gentry. On occasion it could now as a group relish — within the narrow limits of the unsubversive and the uncontroversial — the plaints of its liberals against "the bureaucracy," their pleas for agriculture and local autonomy. That this *rapprochement* endured is explainable only by the coincidence of two different developments: on the one hand, the large antiliberal segment of the gentry had temporarily withdrawn from public affairs, and, on the other, all the more or less oppositional elements of the whole class were now syphoned and concentrated in one institution — the new self-government.

II

Initiated in 1864 for the countryside, this new institution of local self-government was designated the *zemstvo* after ancient Russian usage. Like Prussia's comparable *Landtag*, this word may best be translated as "territorial assembly."

The zemstvo was the most extensive and autonomous

form of self-government in Russian history. Peter the Great and half a century later Catherine II had made gestures in this direction. But the resulting schemes centered on separate corporate organizations of different estates or classes. And they were sickly growths that did not lead to any new tradition of independence or initiative in relation to the paternalistic central government. The zemstvo was to be "all-class" (*vsesoslovnoe*), composed of elected representatives of all estates, and its jurisdiction was larger than that of the earlier schemes.

Some three dozen provinces in European Russia were allowed by the government to establish zemstvos, the less Russian areas all being excluded. These provinces (*guberniia*) were broken up into approximately 400 smaller districts (*uezd*). In both provinces and districts, the zemstvo consisted of two bodies: (1) an assembly of delegates (*glasnye*), which met annually and was elected for three-year terms; and (2) a permanent, salaried executive body, the zemstvo board, whose members were elected by the respective zemstvo assemblies, likewise for a three-year term.

The electorate of the zemstvo comprised three separate categories: the towns, the peasant communes, and all individual landowners, including non-nobility. Representation was proportional to land ownership, which meant that urban representation was sparse. The constituency elected the delegates to the lower, district assemblies by indirect methods. In the case of the peasant communes, the already existing canton (*volost*) councils elected the delegates, while the landowners chose electoral colleges for the same purpose. Delegates to the higher, province assemblies were elected by the district zemstvo assemblies from among their own members, regardless of class. In the first set of elections, during the 1860's, the number of district delegates totaled almost 12,000 and that of province delegates, over 2,000. More than 1,200 members of zemstvo boards were also elected. From the outset, the nobility — and its most numerous group, the gentry — predominated in the zemstvo. Nor was this surprising. Even before the Great Reforms, the nobility had enjoyed a near-monopoly of local offices. Afterward, it continued to be the most privileged class in local as in national affairs. By the zemstvo statute of 1864 each marshal of the nobility, an influential local leftover of Catherine II's corporate self-government, became the ex officio chairman of his district or province zemstvo assembly. Peasant electors were free to choose their delegates from other classes, and occasionally — sometimes with outside pressure — they elected landowners. Above all, education, self-confidence, and social status gave the nobility a pre-eminence that neither the peasantry nor the small town bourgeoisie in the zemstvo ever sought to challenge.

Statistics dramatize the nobility's hegemony, showing that the nobility as a whole held 42 per cent of the district assembly seats, and that it was still more numerous in the province assemblies (74 per cent) and in zemstvo boards (62 per cent) where estates did not vote separately, as they did in the lower, district assemblies. Over the years, the gentry's hold over the zemstvo remained so strong that it retained the same percentage of district seats for three decades, although during that period (1860's–1890's) its landholdings shrank by almost one third.[1]

What were the functions of this novel institution, dominated as it was by the nobility? The zemstvo had partial or complete jurisdiction over several areas of local rural life:

Education — particularly primary schooling. The zemstvo shared this leading concern with the Ministry of Public Education, the parochial schools, and the peasant communes. The building and maintenance of schools were augmented by the zemstvo through the training of teachers, preparation of textbooks, and adult vocational courses for peasants on agronomy, machinery, and the like.

Welfare — above all health, through a network of hospitals, dispensaries, first-aid stations; also life and fire insurance, veterinary service, saving banks, famine relief, soil conservation.

Administration — the maintenance and construction of local roads, assistance to prisons and postal services, elaborate statistical surveys.

Before the Great Reforms, before the 1860's, many of these activities had been controlled by the individual nobleman-landowner in his manorial jurisdiction over his serfs. Most of the remainder had been vested in the nobility's own units of self-government. Still others had been part of the government apparatus — or had not been organized at all. Now all these innumerable local activities converged in a new institution subject to popularly elected representatives and officers. This was indeed one of the major transformations of recent Russian history. It is not surprising that the enthusiastic expectations of some were soon matched by bitter opposition from others in the gentry and also in the government.

"Ambivalent" probably best describes the government's attitude toward its own recent progeny. As an entirely new form of rural self-government, the zemstvo was bound to arouse the expectation, joyous or apprehensive, that from the local level it might expand to the national, that it would be the "building" to which a parliament would be the logical "roof." In the deliberations before 1864, such hopes were voiced by Alexander II himself and by a number of high officials. Ere long, the "building-roof" analogy of a zemstvo structure capped by a parliament became ubiquitous in constitutionalist thought and in its agitational appeals. The government's own plans originally gave the zemstvo sweeping autonomy and jurisdiction, but as early as 1864, when the new self-government was officially promulgated, the tide had turned and a countercurrent had set in. Although the original scheme was not dropped, it was modified here and there. Where previously the zemstvo was to enjoy a minor share of politics and even of power, these were categorically proscribed from 1864 on. Individually zemstvos were permitted to take up only routine and technical matters. Any talk of politics and national affairs in zemstvo addresses or petitions was condemned, rejected, on occasion punished.

As a result, it became less and less clear whether the zemstvo was to be a self-governing part of the state structure or a separate government-chartered corporation — or merely a private philanthropic association. Since different ministries, court circles, and ideological currents within the government disagreed and wavered, this question was never settled, and the zemstvo's ambiguous status persisted. As occurs frequently in the life of any bureaucratized autocracy, the zemstvo and its multifarious activities shifted from day to day, subject to the chicaneries or favors — and apathy — of individual officials high and low.

At the outset, the government exercised direct control over the zemstvo by means of a suspensive veto by the local governor and of government approval of most financial decisions — decisions the more important since the zemstvo was expected to support itself by taxing its own constituency. In succeeding years, these original controls over local self-government were repeatedly augmented. The additional restrictions spelled still less autonomy and still less politics:

1866 — Zemstvo taxation of local industry and commerce is limited.

1867 — The jurisdiction of zemstvo assemblies and the contact between individual zemstvos is circumscribed, and the governor's approval is required for publishing zemstvo proceedings.

1869 — Zemstvos are required to put postage on their mails, a minor gesture to emphasize their nongovernmental status.

1879 — The main supervisory role over local education is assigned to the marshals of the nobility, with very limited representation for the zemstvos.

1889 — Zemstvo autonomy is considerably reduced by the abandonment of a parallel innovation of the Great Reforms: the previously zemstvo-elected justice of the peace (*mirovoi sudia*) is replaced by a government official (*zemskii nachalnik*), who combines legal with increased administrative jurisdiction over the peasants.

1890 — In the first over-all substitution for the 1864 statute,

1. all members of zemstvo boards become government officials subject to approval by the governor;
2. the Ministry of the Interior, and the governor

as its local representative, are given increased authority to veto zemstvo decisions and to punish board members;

3. the government now appoints the peasantry's delegates to zemstvo assemblies, from lists of candidates submitted by the peasant electors;
4. peasant representation is sharply reduced;
5. only landowners are allowed to be chairmen of zemstvo boards.

This woeful chronology was not accidental. It was bound up with the zemstvo's ambivalent status between self-governing state institution and private philanthropy, with the local friction between zemstvo and government officials, with growing state interference in zemstvo affairs, and — uppermost — with the general belief that the government could crush the zemstvo just as readily, and singlehandedly, as it had originally decreed that institution out of nowhere. All of this encouraged gentry absenteeism and apathy toward the zemstvo, a situation that often left the field to the liberal minority, enabling it to dominate the zemstvo with or without passive peasant support.

The left-right battles in the zemstvo focused on varying issues. In the 1860's the paramount question was most frequently the nature and sources of the zemstvo's self-taxation; in the 1870's it was the zemstvo's role in education; in the 1880's, the size of its budget and hence of its activities. But regardless of the issue, these battles revolved around the same basic zemstvo problems: relation to the government, expansion of activities, aid to the peasantry rather than the landowners.

II

During this gray, unspectacular era, the liberals lacked an organization, an uncensored journal, a clear-cut program, and an identifiable group of theorists or spokesmen. They rightly felt that they were on the defensive, and usually they operated locally and *ad hoc,* truly deserving in this period the appellation "empiricists par excellence." [2]

In the zemstvo Russian liberalism had acquired its foremost "nonpolitical" arena, a substitute for open political activities which the state itself monopolized. After the vastly exaggerated expectations of the Great Reforms era, the liberals cooled toward the zemstvo during the sixties, when its lack of genuine autonomy became unmistakable. Although the liberals had few if any alternatives to the zemstvo, only the late 1870's initiated a new era of liberal enthusiasm. It was less dreamy and intense, more concrete and prosaic than the excitements of the Great Reforms. From then until the 1905 Revolution, liberals directed their enthusiasm and loyalty to the zemstvo as the principal means of furthering their aims.

A unique arena for "nonpolitical" politics had thus been established and recognized as such, and a loose assortment of independently wealthy notables was ready to take advantage of it. But what would they seek to do in the zemstvo and why?

First and last, the liberal notables continued to be noblemen, landowners, gentlemen-farmers or gentlemen of leisure. This did not mean that they could not be rebels or visionaries or activists. But it meant that the gentry notables who embraced the "small deeds" liberalism of this era were themselves people who lived a comfortable, tranquil life — a life in which domestic enjoyments overshadowed cosmic philosophies, a life which they were not tempted to forfeit. These men divided their time between their estates, their residences in Moscow or St. Petersburg, and spas in Western Europe. Sons of the gentry had begun to study for the professions and to work at them full-time, but in terms of liberal politics this group did not loom large until the end of the century. Rather, the liberal notable usually felt free to abandon himself to the kind of local volunteer activity that Russian society and his own style of life and outlook favored.

Within this rather snug existence, the liberal gentry faced one problem in particular: how to recruit support from below as well as from above. In the middle of the nineteenth century, the most fashionable approach to this problem among Russia's educated minority was provided by populism. This "love of the people" was not confined to the radicals with their agrarian socialism and dreams of peasant revolution. More broadly, populism centered on the belief that Russia's future depended on "the people," the illiterate, drastically backward peasantry — and on raising the material and cultural level of "the people." This task could be accomplished only by the enlightened educated minority. And, under the circumstances, the task must take the form of minute, slow, unspectacular educational and welfare work. Politics, national affairs, reforms must wait.

This nonpolitical *Kulturträger* populism remained a characteristic of the small deeds phase between the 1860's and the 1890's. Its typically Enlightenment reliance on education and humanitarianism, as well as its political motives, were reinforced by economic considerations. For after the agricultural crisis had started in the 1870's, a well-off peasantry became essential for a gentry eager to assure debt repayments and to sell its own land profitably. A complementary economic motive applied in particular to the least agricultural central provinces of European Russia. There a better skilled and more educated peasantry would be likely to squeeze out more income from the barren soil, as well as from the growing handicrafts enterprises and factories.

If the liberal gentry's populism did not call for political action, neither did its other principal approach in the small deeds era. This was the liberals' attempt to win support from above by persuading Russia's illiberal government — in its own terms — that the country, the people, the liberals themselves had earned the reforms the liberals advocated.

In modern times man has tended to regard such unheroic expediency, such prosaic accommodation, with much less favor than he regards wars and revolution, and to condemn it as appeasement. Yet as the nineteenth century grew older, as revolutions throughout Europe boomeranged — either through terror or restoration — against their liberal initiators, and as the status quo took on many liberal features, liberalism in general leaned more and more toward accommodation with the status quo. Like Western liberals, the Russian liberal notables, too, appealed for compromise, gradualism, reasonableness, nonviolence. This mood was not difficult to explain or to defend: politics as such had been proscribed by the state; government dissolution of the zemstvo was a constant threat; an overly oppositional liberalism might lose its backers in the gentry; and, perhaps most important, support from below — whether through spontaneous mass unrest or through the long-range campaign of *Kulturträger* populism — seemed far off. All these stated and unstated considerations explain why small deeds liberalism courted support from above as well as from below. This is why the liberals participated, or even led, when the gentry as a whole and the zemstvo addressed the government in terms of jingo patriotism and monarchist ardor, terms that provoked the satiric comment from Saltykov-Shchedrin's *Fables* which serves as an epigraph for this chapter.

Whether the circumstances and the mood of the period favored *Kulturträger* populism or government accommodation, what was called for was nonpolitical activity, to which nothing was better adapted than local self-government. Restricted to the nonpolitical realm of local education, welfare, and administration, the zemstvo offered unparalleled and officially sanctioned contact with "the people," with the peasant mass of the population. And what better showcase for popular maturity, for national loyalty, and above all for liberal moderation and utility could be devised than a tsar-given, nearly nation-wide institution?

The two facets of small deeds Russian liberalism — courting support equally from below and above, in each case through local, nonpolitical means — were clearly articulated as early as the 1860's. The great liberal writer Turgenev, in a letter to the partly liberal, partly radical Alexander Herzen, warned him and his radical friends that they

despise and trample on the educated class on Russia, while supposing that revolutionary or reformatory elements exist in the people. In reality, quite the opposite is true. Revolution — in the true and concrete meaning of the word [the moderate constitutionalism of 1789]; I might say, in the largest meaning — exists only in the minority of the educated class; and this is quite sufficient for its triumph, if only we do not extirpate ourselves by our mutual quarrels. . . . The role of the educated class in Russia is to transmit civilization to the people, in order that they may themselves hereafter decide what they will accept or repudiate . . . and this role is not yet played out. . . . In fact, you are brought to repudiate revolution, because the people you worship are conservative par excellence; in their sheepskins, their warm and dirty hovels they foster the germs of a bourgeoisie which will leave the ill-famed western bourgeoisie far behind.[3]

The conviction that an illiberal government might grant liberal reforms, but only after much proof of loyalty as well as usefulness, was reiterated by *S.-Peterburgskie vedomosti*, the leading organ of the liberal gentry:

At the moment that the zemstvo institutions have grown strong and have acquired the final confidence of the government through conscientious execution of its tasks on a strictly legal basis — at that moment, probably, the zemstvo will not be refused the [governmental] acceptance of this higher body ["all-Russian zemstvo," or parliament] to the extent that the government considers it essential to the interests of the whole people.[4]

Beyond the united front of small deeds, however, the liberal gentry began to divide into ideological currents Having gradually become dormant since the slavophile — westernizer polemics of the mid-century, these differences did not re-emerge until the closing decade of the century. As yet — between the Great Reforms and the 1890's — the differences were neither passionate nor entirely clear-cut. Most of the gentry liberals still belonged ideologically to an amorphous middle group that believed firmly in gradualism, in legal and nonrevolutionary opposition. It shared with most Western liberals of this period the apprehensions about unqualified democracy and large-scale social reforms. And it admired Western parliaments and constitutions without being certain when and how they might be transplanted to Russia.

Typical of this group was a major but solitary figure: Boris Chicherin, an aristocrat, a zemstvo leader, a devout Hegelian, and a prolific scholar in philosophy and legal theory. Akin to the *Rechtsstaat* liberals of Bismarck Germany, Chicherin insisted far more on laws and legality than on parliamentary (or popular) sovereignty. This explains the bizarre phenomenon of Chicherin's occasional fraternizing with Konstantin Pobedonostsev, the ardently antiliberal ideologist of the status quo, at the same time that he propagated his own variety of liberalism. That Chicherin did favor limited monarchy, and not autocracy, he illustrated at great length in 1866, in a theoretical work on political systems, *O narodnom predstavitelstve*. In this work Chicherin attacked autocracy as much as democracy, and reiterated his characteristic emphasis on moderation, gradualism, reforms from above. This position is confirmed by a prominent public address of 1882, in which, accepting his election as mayor [*golova*] of Moscow by its municipal duma, Chicherin urged:

Above all, let us constantly remember that at the moment the Russian state is not in a normal condition. Only through harmonious actions of the government and the public can we defeat the malady hovering over us [terrorism by revolutionaries] and shape a brighter future for our fatherland. I am convinced, gentlemen, that acting in this fashion we shall lose nothing. On the contrary, only this way shall we advance the public cause. And the time will come when the government itself, seeing in us not the elements of ferment but a defense of order, will feel the need to broaden the narrow area of local self-government and to bring the public into the general structure of the Russian state. [We should] not irritate [it] by rushing toward this time, not come out prematurely with immoderate or ill-timed demands or with claims that go beyond the area of activity given to us. To avoid this, to await confidently the decision of the supreme authority, and to show ourselves worthy of the high calling by peaceable activity for public benefit — this, in my opinion, should be our policy.[5]

In Russia, Rechtsstaat liberalism recruited few articulate spokesmen, however. By the turn of the century the younger liberals had excommunicated Chicherin as "conservative." Yet isolated as Chicherin himself was most of the time, his formula of reforming the status quo from within was at least until the 1890's more palatable and more accepted than was outright constitutionalism. This is why the Great Reforms were so idealized, why such transformations from above served as the symbol for most small deeds liberals. These men hoped to see the Great Reforms completed by the government itself, rather than by the population, backward and potentially turbulent as it was.

IV

The question of long-range goals did not involve this amorphous middle group, however. Two other currents arose that in effect represented the minimum program and at the maximum program of Russian liberalism during its small deeds phase. To the right of the middle group, and hence representing the liberals' minimum program, were some slavophiles of this period. Like their illustrious philosophizing forerunners of the mid-century, these slavophiles espoused an idealized version of absolute monarchy. They, too, believed that Russia represented a unique society, drastically different from what was condemned as the West's materialism, atomization, and legalism. In their Romantic blueprint, an agrarian and deeply religious society should ideally be linked "by mutual trust" — a favorite phrase — to a paternalistic, enlightened despot. This royal paterfamilias would be advised not by officials but by a consultative assembly of his most esteemed subjects: the *zemskii sobor* (territorial congress), a passing phenomenon in Russian history which, two centuries after its demise, the slavophiles sought to resuscitate and embellish.

Disagreeing both with the government and with its constitutionalist opponents, the slavophile liberals asserted fervently that complete self-government locally could and should be combined with autocracy at the top. But while they rejected two traditional objectives of political liberalism — constitution and parliament — they continued to hold the early slavophiles' other liberal ideals. Thus they represented a definitely individualistic and humanitarian opposition to arbitrary government, absence of individual rights, and the reliance of the emperor on "the bureaucracy" instead of on "the people."

In retrospect, these liberal slavophiles of the later nineteenth century have been overshadowed by their more famous and dramatic contemporaries, such as Dostoevski, Danilevski, Pobedonostsev — nationalists who are often considered slavophiles. But in the nobility, at least, it is debatable whether it was the nationalists or the liberal slavophiles who had the greater influence at the time.

The one early figure who did not share the original

slavophiles' predilection for theoretical writings and discourses on theology and the philosophy of history was Aleksandr Koshelev. This lifelong intimate of Aleksei Khomiakov and Ivan Kireevski had come, like the leading slavophile theorists, from the well-off provincial nobility. He was one of the most prolific and outspoken publicists of the decades before and after the Great Reforms. He served as publisher of several slavophile and liberal periodicals: *Russkaia beseda* in the 1850's, *Beseda* in the 1870's, *Zemstvo* in the early 1880's. A steady stream of articles, memoranda, and pamphlets on current events flowed from Koshelev's pen. When censorship prevented their publication in Russia, he published them abroad, sending copies to the tsar with a courteous and proper note — and each time he went unpunished.

In addition to being a noted publicist, Koshelev stood out as an example of the eternal activist among the gentry notables. Dividing his time between a winter house in Moscow and a profitable estate near Riazan, he served at one time or another in the following capacities: district marshal of the nobility, member of several governmental commissions editing the Emancipation Act, Russian finance director in Poland for two years, long-term member of the district and province zemstvo assemblies in Riazan, justice of the peace, chairman of his district school council, member of the Moscow municipal duma.

Ideologically, Koshelev identified himself completely with the early slavophiles. But partly because he outlived them and partly because of his preoccupation with politics rather than philosophy, Koshelev regarded himself almost as much a liberal as a slavophile. He boasted that the slavophiles were actually more liberal than the liberals in the battle for an equitable Emancipation Act, that they fought hardest for all of the Great Reforms, that they never attacked liberals or liberalism. By the 1870's he dissociated himself from the "ossified" slavophiles who persisted in the passé polemic against westernizers and were too antiliberal.[6] Although, as a slavophile, Koshelev continued to oppose constitutionalism, his advocacy of the immediate convocation of a popularly elected national consultative assembly, his equally ardent attacks on "the bureaucracy," and his defense of the zemstvo placed him close to most liberals of his later days, following the Great Reforms of the 1860's.[7]

If the pamphleteering activist, Koshelev, belonged to the original slavophiles, a later generation supplied the leader of the slavophile liberals. This was Dmitri Shipov, one of the two most influential figures among the gentry liberals at the turn of the century. Born in mid-century of a gentry family near Moscow, Shipov devoted himself to agriculture there. At only twenty-six he was elected a delegate to the zemstvo assemblies of his own district and also of the Moscow province. The year 1891 saw his election as chairman of his district's zemstvo board, and two years later he assumed what amounted to the most prominent position in the entire zemstvo world: the chairmanship of the zemstvo board of the province of Moscow, the most central and eminent in all Russia. This post he occupied for eleven stormy and busy years, until he was removed by government orders a year before the 1905 Revolution. During his tenure he initiated a number of important zemstvo conferences, became one of the leading technical experts on the zemstvo and acted as spokesman for that institution before ministers and other government officials. Shipov's personal behavior was characterized by earnestness and a brooding moralism rather than by militancy or charisma. In his face[8] spectacles and the usual beard seemed to disguise reserve and even shyness, and a quiet rather than stormy self-confidence. True to slavophile principles, Shipov repeatedly opposed constitutions:

> The constitutional theory aims at the limitation of the rights of state authority and the extension of the rights of popular representation. It thus seems to raise to a principle the system of inevitable rivalry and struggle between [government authority and popular representation]. This principle contradicts my entire view of life. I am convinced that a fruitful interaction between authority and popular representation is possible only with their moral solidarity, with the realization and execution by both sides of their moral duty.[9]

During the 1905 Revolution Shipov's views were restated and elaborated:

> what are we to do once we acknowledge the unfitness of the system ruling up to now? It should not, we think, be replaced by a new "contrived" one. The task is to remove from the system that which made it unfit. And what made it unfit was the separation of the tsar from the people, the lack of access to the tsar of the voice of the population. To put it more bluntly, it was the bureaucracy's limitation of the sovereign imperial authority. From this point of view, what is desirable is a renovated imperial authority on the one hand and on the other free access to the tsar of the people's voice through elected representatives.[10]

Although Shipov's opposition to constitutional government, together with his warm espousal of the nonindividualistic peasant commune and an idealized autocracy, placed him with the slavophiles, he voiced some definite qualifications of their position: "If I feel a deep respect for the slavophile doctrine, which has as its basis a deep realization of the moral-religious duty imposed on people . . . I do not fully share the attitude of the slavophiles to the slogans: orthodoxy, autocracy, and nationality." [11]

Shipov explained that he did not believe in the unqualified superiority of Orthodox Christianity over other religions. According to his view autocracy was not god-given, nor should it be absolute. And, although he agreed with the slavophiles that historically the Russian people might have developed differently from the people of Western Europe, he did not hold that they were unique or had a universal mission to perform. These major qualifications to the original slavophile doctrine all pointed in a liberal direction. But Shipov's ideology remained in essence close to that of the slavophile theorists. They shared a common general suspicion of constitutionalism and its Western European manifestations, a particular opposition to the constitutionalists' rationalism and legalism, and a deeply religious and moral emphasis.

Many of Shipov's beliefs estranged him from other liberals, and in a different time and place he might not have been categorized as a liberal at all. But this term is very much a matter of local usage, of a specific political spectrum. Decisive for Russian liberals of the small deeds period was Shipov's attitude toward the zemstvo. As might be expected, the moral and humanitarian meaning of the zemstvo is uppermost for Shipov. A speech in 1898 is typical: "the foundation of this association [the zemstvo] is undoubtedly moral — the foundation of mutual help based on the duty of Christian love. Proceeding from this foundation, zemstvo institutions . . . concentrate their activities and their means on aiding the neediest classes and localities to meet their existing requirements." In general, Shipov and his slavophile followers idealized local self-government and personal liberties, with England the usual symbol,[12] as much as they did autocracy and the *zemskii sobor*. As a result, their typically slavophile moralism was paralleled by a stubborn insistence that the zemstvo — and Russia as a whole — could not flourish without greater freedom.

As a vigorous and communal undertaking, the zemstvo can proceed and develop successfuly only if the necessary independence is guaranteed to it. We zemstvo people believe deeply that local needs can be met only with the broad development of independent public activities — [independent activities] within the framework of the historically developed government system in Russia.[13]

Shipov's closing phrase underlined the limitations of slavophile liberalism. He insisted on freedom for independent, nongovernmental activities — but only on the local level, and within the framework of the existing autocracy. The basis of this qualification was the slavophile's Romantic idealization of autocracy, an autocracy to be far more enlightened and nonbureaucratized than the Russian monarchy of Shipov's own day. This discrepancy between ideal and reality helps to explain not only Shipov's repeated wavering but also his outspoken, at times seemingly reckless, attacks on the monarchy for failing to live up to its own standards. Such a position had little appeal for more advanced liberals. But for the less liberal majority of the gentry, and for the government too, Shipov's brand of liberalism (like Chicherin's) then seemed less brash and more persuasive. But Shipov, like Chicherin, never ceased craving some increase of liberties for the individual and his

private and local organizations — and never ceased blue-
printing reforms to introduce and institutionalize these liberties. This, if nothing else, is what distinguished even the
most moderate liberal from the conservative, who preferred
or even idealized the status quo.

V

As far to the left of the middle group as the slavophiles
were to the right were the constitutionalists. This rival
ideological current comprised the maximum program of
Russian gentry liberalism. The slavophile liberals wanted
individual and group freedom within an idealized autocracy; the amorphous middle group may have sought greater
changes, but only cautiously and legally. The constitutionalists, however, wanted still more and at a quicker pace.
Moreover, while the slavophiles favored laws and other controls to bridle the government officials, the constitutionalists'
maximum program sought to subject the monarch as well
to enforceable rules of law. By definition this meant abolish-
ing autocracy altogether rather than purifying it, as the
slavophile liberals wanted. In the early decades of gentry
liberalism, before the 1890's, the constitutionalists were the
least numerous and the least influential of the three groups.
But in the 1890's, as times became more turbulent and new
allies appeared on the scene, this group assumed the leadership of gentry liberalism.

The constitutionalists and the middle group shared a belief in constitutions, in a sovereign parliament, in the supremacy of laws over men, in local self-government not as
an end itself but as the "building" that would support a
parliamentary "roof." All of this the slavophile liberals
questioned or denied. Elsewhere, however, the middle
group found itself closer to the slavophiles than to the

constitutionalists. An example is the disagreement over the great liberal dilemma in all nonliberal countries: whether to seek change from above or below — and how. Most of the time, the Russian gentry's amorphous liberal middle tended to go along with the slavophiles in seeking changes from the monarch, and in fearing or discounting changes wrought from below. Important here was a common faith in legality, a common dislike of clandestine action and of revolutionaries. The constitutionalists disagreed with them about both tactics and strategy. For them, the main hope of reform came from below, not from above; and in the seeking of mass support, neither clandestine activities nor revolutionaries were at all repellent.

The logic of this position pushed the constitutionalists into a realm avoided by other gentry liberals, the realm of social reform and of greater democracy. Slowly but surely, the Russian constitutionalists developed a position quite similar to that of Clemenceau and his French Radicals of the same period, the turn of the century. In Russia, as in France, the need to compete with socialists for mass support was combined with a conscious, belligerent rejection of the earlier liberals' reluctance to use the state to assure social welfare and social equality. It is this new welfare liberalism, of which John Stuart Mill and Gladstone were the hesitant forerunners and Clemenceau and Lloyd George the early tribunes, that developed among Russia's constitutionalists.

If any one place in Russia served as the birthplace of constitutionalism, it was Tver. Situated almost as close to St. Petersburg as to Moscow, the city of Tver was typical of the least fertile central provinces of European Russia. Since the 1850's Tver had been the center of the most vocal and the best-known gentry constitutionalists. Ironically, among Tver's outstanding liberals were several younger brothers of the world-renowned revolutionary Mikhail Bakunin, himself passionately antiliberal. Through him and through other links, the entire Bakunin family from the 1830's on had been close to such great radicals as Herzen and Belinski. The Bakunin group of Tver constitutionalists represented a kindred liberalism, with an emphasis on economic and political democracy.

A grand climax at Tver came after the public and heated nation-wide disputes in the 1850's on the nature of peasant emancipation. In these disputes, the Tver gentry assumed — and voiced — the most radical position. When, in 1859, the government forbade provincial assemblies of the nobility to "enter into any kind of deliberations on matters pertaining to the peasant question," the Tver assembly voted 231 to 56 to ask the tsar to reopen such discussions. And when the government responded by removing from office the liberal marshal of the nobility, A. M. Unkovski, Tver countered by establishing twelve Unkovski scholarships at the University of Moscow and by refusing to elect a successor. After an uneasy peace with the government, the Tver gentry erupted again in its first assembly of the nobility after the Emancipation Act had been promulgated; at this meeting in February 1862, it threw a bombshell in the form of a resolution adopted by a majority of 102 to 24.

This sensational and much quoted Tver resolution of 1862 broke precedent not only in demanding drastic political reforms through a popularly elected national assembly, but also — reminiscent of the French Revolution — in proclaiming the renunciation of all class privileges by the Tver nobility. It thus ventured into social reforms, an area even less frequented by the nobility than the sphere of sweeping political transformations. The resolution opened with a demand for a popularly controlled government administration, a free court, and full publicity in all state and public activities. It included a condemnation of the Emancipation Act for merely raising, rather than solving, the question of freeing the peasantry. Then came the two key passages:

The nobility, being deeply imbued by a consciousness of the urgent need to overcome this antagonism [between estates] and wishing to destroy any possibility of the reproach that it represents an obstacle in the path of general welfare, proclaims before all Russia that it renounces all the privileges of its estate. . . .

Moving from social to political reforms, the Tver assembly coolly brushed aside the usual liberal plea for the government to initiate and execute the proposed reform. Instead, a second key passage went even beyond the call for a national duma by the slavophile Koshelev:

The realization of these reforms is impossible through government measures by which our society has evolved thus far. Even assuming the full readiness of the government to carry out the reforms, the nobility is filled with the profound conviction that the government is not in a condition to carry them out. For this reason the nobility does not turn to the government with a plea to promulgate these reforms, but recognizing its inadequacy in this matter, limits itself to indicating the path on which it must enter to save itself and society. This path is an assembly of elected representatives of the whole people, without distinguishing between estates.[14]

The Tver nobility took no further action beyond transmitting to the government its remarkably radical and

brusque resolutions. But in condemning the Emancipation
Act, Tver had voiced the political resentment of the whole
nobility against administrative "revolutions from above,"
current in all the major autocracies of Europe. These enabled
the state and its professional administrators to impose economic and political modernization on recalcitrant or backward classes. Russia's aristocracy and gentry could thus join
in denigrating this method of freeing their serfs. Moreover,
in that central region of European Russia the nobles' estates
and their class privileges were less profitable and less important to them than to the nobility elsewhere. It was natural that provinces such as Tver early became liberal
strongholds, while the black soil provinces favored either
the status quo or a landlord oligarchy — at least until the
government's industrial neomercantilism of the 1890's.[15]

Yet why did Tver support the political and social demands of the constitutionalists more often and more actively
than any other place in Russia? To political vexation and
economic motives must be added proximity to both Moscow
and St. Petersburg, as well as an unusual galaxy of liberal
leaders like the younger Bakunin brothers. Important, too,
was the long-time leader of the constitutionalists and eventually Shipov's one rival as leader of all the liberal gentry
— Ivan Petrunkevich.

Petrunkevich's life, like Shipov's, began in the middle
of the century in the family of a gentry landowner. Again
akin to Shipov, Petrunkevich while only in his twenties became a delegate to his South Russian (Chernigov) district
and province zemstvo assemblies, and also justice of the
peace. But while, in the case of Shipov, these posts were
followed by long tenure in the key executive position of
zemstvo board chairman, Petrunkevich's more radical activities led to his being banished from his native province. The

new home base at which he settled in the 1880's was Tver. Even before moving to Tver, Petrunkevich was bound to the pivotal Bakunin family "by deep friendship and family relation" (Petrunkevich's brother had married a Bakunin). In his earliest organizational attempts he received the strongest backing from the Tver liberals, with whom he shared a reverence for Herzen; from his boyhood on, Petrunkevich recalls in his memoirs, "Herzen's ideas remained dear to me throughout my life. More than that, they determined my direction in political and social questions. Since then more than sixty years have passed, but I still consider him my guide." [16]

By 1890 Petrunkevich had become a delegate to Tver's district and province assemblies, and an intimate member of the Tver liberal circle. Unlike Shipov, however, Petrunkevich regarded the zemstvo only as a means, an arena for his restless and unceasing proselytizing. Not a brooding *moraliste* or prosaic administrator like Shipov, Petrunkevich was rather the rebel and the agitator. His public career was punctuated by explosive orations as well as stubborn defenses of his own militant views. His face,[17] too, with its belligerent, protruding lips and small, sharp eyes, showed little of Shipov's reserve and tranquillity.

Petrunkevich's ideology, and that of the constitutionalists in the gentry before the 1890's, emerged in a series of unprecedented actions and statements. All of these Petrunkevich himself initiated in the late 1870's, when he was in his thirties and still unknown.

Petrunkevich first assumed the leading role he retained until 1905 in the closing years of the 1870's, when Russia witnessed the one political revival between the Great Reforms and the 1890's. It occurred under significant and familiar circumstances — after a war (the Russo-Turkish War of 1877–1878) and after widespread unrests caused by the terrorism of a small group of revolutionary populists. Following two major assassinations, the second that of the chief of gendarmes, the government issued an appeal for public support against the terror.

On his own initiative, Petrunkevich thereupon attempted to organize and co-ordinate constitutionalist zemstvo replies to the government appeal. His first move was to address a public dinner of zemstvo and professional leaders in Kharkov in November 1878. He declared that the public must be opposed to terror from above as much as to terror from below, and that the government must recognize that the only cure was a public life based on law and free expression. Following this — and again on his own — Petrunkevich did something unprecedented in the annals of gentry liberalism: he attempted to establish collaboration between liberals and revolutionaries. This he did at a conspiratorial Kiev meeting with five leaders of the revolutionary terrorists. One of the revolutionaries present has described how Petrunkevich

developed the thought that a constitutional reform was necessary for Russia and would be useful to all Russian groups, including the socialists, since it would create greater scope for activity. As a conclusion from this, he suggested that all groups unite to attain a constitution. In his opinion, all legal means — submission of petitions, peaceful demonstrations, and so on — should be tried first. In order to attract more people into the movement, it was planned to develop strong agitation in the public through the press. Pamphlets of a constitutionalist nature, which due to censorship conditions could not be printed inside Russia, the zemstvo man [Petrunkevich] would have printed abroad and from there delivered by contraband means. . . . All these were thoughts with which our terrorists probably would have agreed if it was not for one point. In the opinion of the zemstvo man, one of the first prerequisites for constitutional agitation was the suspension of the revolutionaries' terrorist activities.[18]

After the rejection of Petrunkevich's unique bid to the revolutionaries, the third of his singlehanded ventures took place in his own zemstvo assembly, meeting at Chernigov in January 1879, to reply to the government appeal for public support. Petrunkevich had been commissioned to draft the reply, and his draft was approved overwhelmingly by an informal advance meeting of the zemstvo delegates. But meanwhile, as a consequence of the earlier, Petrunkevich-inspired Kharkov address, the Minister of the Interior had issued orders against such addresses. Hence a dramatic session of the assembly saw Chernigov's marshal of the nobility — as ex officio chairman of the zemstvo assembly — close the stormy meeting before Petrunkevich's draft could be read in full and voted upon.

Expressing complete loyalty to tsar and country, the Chernigov address emphasized that ideas cannot be fought by repression, and that profound social changes had occurred in Russia since the Great Reforms. It then pointed to three major causes of unrest: "the nature of secondary and higher educational institutions; the absence of freedom of speech and press; the absence of legality in Russian life." The address emphasized that "the struggle with subversive ideas will be possible only if the public has the appropriate means. These means are freedom of speech [and] press, freedom of opinion, and free science." The zemstvos in particular lacked the means to reach the government, to publish their own views, even to meet with each other. And, the address went on, the Great Reforms were incomplete, their achievements having been undermined by constant changes. The conclusion of the Chernigov address was reminiscent of the Tver resolution of 1862: "Therefore the zemstvo of the Chernigov province notes with inexpressible regrets its complete inability to take any practical measures whatsoever in the struggle against evil, and considers it its civic duty to inform the government accordingly." [19]

The Chernigov address concentrated unmistakably on personal liberties and zemstvo autonomy, the two demands of the slavophile liberals' minimum program. It omitted any mention of constitution or parliament, not to speak of basic social and economic reforms. Petrunkevich himself has offered two explanations for this. At the time he commented that "the Chernigov zemstvo could not say more than what it did say, probably wishing to unite in one common protest the largest possible number of voices and trends." This makes very good sense, but in retrospect Petrunkevich himself offered a second explanation that is equally plausible: "after the Chernigov experience there could be no doubt that the government was organically incapable of being moderate in anything and of granting a constitution until forced into it by the pressure of circumstances." [20]

Whatever the principal reason why the Chernigov address failed to mention constitutional reforms, a clandestine and anonymous Petrunkevich pamphlet did speak of these reforms in the same year. Exactly what Petrunkevich sought in 1879 became clear in this pamphlet, especially in its remarkable conclusion:

Life is putting forth a number of questions, the solution of which belongs to the zemstvo as the spokesman for the wishes and aspirations of the Russian people. Although the people still believe in the government and count only on it to relieve them of their miseries, although the people do not recognize the zemstvo as the representative of their interests, this is only because the zemstvo has not done anything for them. But as soon as the zemstvo understands completely the necessity of economic reforms; when it takes the whole mass of the people under its protection from the arbitrariness of the police; when it bravely and decisively demands from the government the freedom of speech to discuss its affairs, to watch over the expenditures of national wealth, and make itself inviolable — then the whole people will be on the side of the zemstvo, and its victory will be assured.

But the various questions indicated by us fall into two categories. Some, like freedom of speech and press and personal rights, must be demanded by the zemstvo immediately. Others can be resolved correctly in a general council of representatives of the people. But this council will become the genuine expression of the people's interests only when it is organized by the people itself. Therefore we must not be thought of as actors in a constitutional comedy. Instead, we reject any constitution granted from above and insist on the convening of a constituent assembly.[21]

This, then, was the credo of Petrunkevich, the new leader of gentry constitutionalism. Although the pamphlet was vague about economic and social reforms, its militant spirit was unmistakable. While the Chernigov address had been worded to obtain a maximum of local votes as well as possible publication and transmission to the government, the pamphlet demanded the liberal maximum: a new political order originating not from the government but from a sovereign, popularly elected constituent assembly. The pamphlet repeatedly reiterated the belief that the gentry could not hope to alter Russia's autocracy without shaking the people's ties to it by the gentry's own militant espousal of democracy. A resolute struggle for the twin goals of constitution and democracy — this was Petrunkevich's aim.

In 1879 Petrunkevich took one more step — in addition to the Kharkov speech, the Kiev meeting with the terrorists, the Chernigov address, and the constitutionalist pamphlet. He laid the groundwork, by means of a series of organizing trips, for the first conference of zemstvo constitutionalists. The conference convened in March 1879 in Moscow with 30 or 40 participants. Here is how Petrunkevich described this earliest forerunner of many later gatherings:

All those attending unanimously recognized that only a constitutional order, resting on the force of right and law, can disarm terror and limit the arbitrariness of the authorities. In view of this unanimity of outlook it was decided to organize locally the dissemination of constitutional ideas and to assist all attempts to submit constitutional demands to the government. Lastly it was held essential to conduct such meetings periodically.[22]

But even these modest and concrete plans did not bear fruit. There were no further zemstvo echoes to the liberal, Petrunkevich-inspired resolutions of Kharkov, of Chernigov, and of the perennially "left" Tver. And no direct connection appears to exist between Petrunkevich and the mystifying Zemstvo Union ("Society of Zemstvo Union and Self-government") [28] of 1881–1883.* Within a few weeks of the Moscow gathering, a new spurt of revolutionary terrorism led to stringent police countermeasures that were only later supplemented by the liberal-sounding hints and blueprints of Alexander II's last days. Petrunkevich found himself banished to a comfortable but distant spot, and hence to inactivity. Although he was its only exponent to experience personal punishment, gentry constitutionalism subsided throughout the retrograde 1880's.

VI

Petrunkevich's fast-moving efforts in the late 1870's to promote unity and militancy marked a milestone in Russian liberalism. But the complete failure of these efforts was symptomatic of all the nascent ideological currents in gentry liberalism: of Shipov's slavophiles' minimum program and of the constitutionalists' maximum program, not to mention the ideals of the amorphous liberal mass in between. All were confined to the zemstvo and to nonpolitical small deeds, all were defensive and unorganized, with hazy programs and little ideology. This series of scattered, local rear-guard actions focused on the zemstvo characterized Russian liberalism from the 1860's to the 1890's. Even the period's leading liberal journal, *Vestnik Evropy*, complained soon after Petrunkevich's efforts:

The upswing in public life is mostly caused not by the mass but by small groups of more active people which do

---

* Proclaiming as its goal "the attainment of political liberty by the peoples of Russia," this once rather controversial organization represented an odd melange of inactivity inside Russia and purported control behind the scenes by ultraconservative courtiers, to which was added the émigré journalism of a Ukrainian, Professor Mikhail Dragomanov. Editor of the Zemstvo Union's organ in Geneva, *Volnoe slovo*, Dragomanov was himself a remarkable mixture of liberalism, socialism, and Ukrainian nationalism.

not multiply very quickly among us. If such a group fore-
gathers in a province and acquires some influence, the
province zemstvo begins to work in a more lively fashion,
too, and calls attention to itself. If the same little group
scatters, the once lively zemstvo falls asleep and drops
back to the rear.[24]

The timorousness and amorphousness of Russian liberalism between the 1860's and 1890's cannot be accounted for
by any one factor. Part of the explanation lies in the gentry.
To be sure, it has been the contention of Marxist as well as
Catholic critics — Harold J. Laski's *Rise of Liberalism* and
Thomas P. Neill's *Rise and Decline of Liberalism* are recent
examples — that liberalism expresses the outlook and aspirations of businessmen, of "the bourgeoisie." There is
truth in this contention. But among European history's
numerous qualifications to this thesis none is more striking
than the landowning nobility's recurrent espousal of liberalism. The Whig liberals of eighteenth-century England, the
Restoration liberals in France, the South German liberals
of the later nineteenth century (not to mention our own
Jeffersonians) — all these were closer to landowners than
to businessmen, each spoke with the accents of the country
rather than the city. In Russia, however, the gentry flirted
with liberalism at the time of its own decline — at a time
when, still pampered by the state, it could no longer imitate
the German Junkers' striking economic modernization and
political offensive in the nineteenth century.

Another explanation is the nature of Russia's autocracy.
Here, as in other European autocracies of the era, the leeway for oppositional activity was sometimes strikingly
great. And it is a safe generalization that in all autocracies
opposition has blossomed and grown strong during those

moments — usually rare — when the state's control of the legitimate use of physical force was for some reason threatened or curtailed. The most frequent cause has been military defeat, or the expectation of such defeat. Another lapse may occur during dynastic or even ministerial changes, as illustrated by the Decembrists in 1825. Revolutionary terror, if widespread, can have a similar effect. So can famine or comparable economic disasters. Thus the Great Reforms were touched off by the coincidence of military defeat and the death of a monarch. From the 1860's to the 1890's, Russia witnessed only one such lapse in the state's monopoly of power. It came between the Russo-Turkish War and the terrorists' assassination of Alexander II in 1881. This one lapse gave Petrunkevich his chance for active proselytizing and organizing. But almost two decades had passed between that period and the last oppositional upswing, and neither the gentry as a whole nor its liberals were prepared to follow Petrunkevich's drastic summons.

So long as the state appeared in full possession of power, another potential source of opposition did not enter into play either. This was the populace as a whole, above all the idealized but submissive Russian peasantry. To begin with, the gentry's small deeds liberalism held only limited appeal for other classes; none of them were culturally developed or politically experienced, and the Russian liberalism of that period did not sweeten its pill by any tempting social or economic demands. When this profound political and cultural lag of all classes except the nobility is seen together with the imposing solidity of the state, the populace's passive and mute behavior seems neither mysterious nor peculiarly Russian.

Under the circumstances, Russia's gentry liberals from the 1860's to the 1890's had no choice but to accommodate the autocracy through Kulturträger small deeds. Only the subsequent weakening of autocracy and the appearance of new oppositional elements could produce a more militant and more political liberalism. Not before the turn of the century did "senseless dreams" move to the fore, starting with those "senseless dreams of the participation of zemstvo representatives in the affairs of internal administration" that the young Nicholas II dismissed so scathingly in 1895. Even then, Russian liberals were still impaled on the horns of their haunting dilemma: in a backward society, can there ever be a third choice between cajoling concessions out of an autocratic state or forcing them through revolutions whose utility (for liberal goals) most nineteen-century liberals came to doubt?

Chapter Two

SONS AND GRANDSONS

I shall be quite ready to agree with you, [Bazarov] added, getting up, when you bring forward a single institution in our present mode of life, in family or in social life, which does not call for complete and unqualified destruction.

Turgenev, *Fathers and Sons*

Well, [Lenin] said, if anyone wants to save the fatherland in the Committee [on] Illiteracy, we won't hinder him.

Krupskaya, *Memories of Lenin*

Neither Turgenev nor Lenin is referring here to the nobility or to the gentry liberals. Both have in mind a different class and a different set of ideas. And it is this new class, and its later ideas, that in the 1890's were weaning Russian liberalism away from its "small deeds" phase and its gentry tradition.

It would be misleading, indeed, to see in Turgenev's much analyzed *Fathers and Sons* merely the eternal cleavage between generations, between the aging and the recklessly young. Nor does the conflict really focus on that notable change in Western intellectual fashions, the mid-century drift from romanticism, idealism, and philosophy to realism, materialism, and the natural sciences. Beneath the cleavage of generations, beyond the conflict of intellectual vogues, an old elite was clashing with a new contender. The noble "father," Nikolai Petrovich Kirsanov, his brother Pavel, even his son Arkadi, found themselves assaulted and challenged. The challenger was Evgeni Bazarov, haughty "son" of a new, a different intelligentsia.

In the 1860's, the composition of Russia's intelligentsia was just undergoing a shift typical of countries beginning to modernize. This was the shift from nobility to commoners, and from the "upper intelligentsia" of well-established academic, governmental, and amateur *literati* to a "lower intelligentsia" of university-educated but plebeian teachers, scientists, civil servants, and journalists. By the end of the century, these "sons" were in turn replaced by the "grandsons": a modern professional middle class, large, plebeianized, and prospering.

I

The "sons" of mid-century Russia differed widely from the Occident's catch-all "bourgeoisie" or its Anglicized equivalent, "the middle class." Yet there is one suggestive similarity. This is their reaction to the traditionalism and caste privileges of the landowning nobility. Bazarov's youthfully combative and acid nihilism had little if anything to do with revolution or socialism or terrorism. Bazarov rebelled against the mores of the predominant class, the nobility, and against its easygoing, pastoral style of life. His own alternative: a puritan earnestness, a "realistic" and "scientific" matter-of-factness and rationalism. Again and again, similar circumstances have produced a similar nonconformist reaction in other countries.

If the analogy ends here, this too is suggestive. In the West, and particularly in the favorite English model, the "rise of the bourgeoisie" meant the rise of the businessman — the merchant, manufacturer, and banker. This rise occurred steadily after the Middle Ages, and industrialization merely expanded and consolidated the influence of business in political and economic life. But as we move eastward, the situation changes. Agriculture and feudalism continued to predominate, commerce and manufacture developed more slowly, and while they did develop the government retained more of the initiative and for a longer time.

As a result, while the businessman on the northern

shores of the Atlantic — and almost nowhere else — became the driving force of a rationalistic, egalitarian, and progress-minded society, it was very different farther east. Here dependence on the state, few customers outside the state, a pampered nobility, and a population economically and culturally backward made the businessman in turn timid, accommodating, often uncultured and politically passive. Thus in Russia, despite the vast industrial advances of the late nineteenth century, the younger scions of big business did not develop political appetites until a decade or two later, on the eve of World War I. Only then — too late — did they seem prepared to risk the state's ever paternalistic bounties by occasional opposition to government policies.

The still prevailing Western custom of interpreting modern history in terms of the business entrepreneur obscures the key role of two other forces, which elsewhere tended to compensate in a peculiar way for the arrested or deformed growth of business. One of these compensating forces is, of course, the state. Even in the Occident it is the state that in the early stages of industrialization and again in the advanced industrialism of the twentieth century plays a dominant role. Farther east, power considerations propelled the otherwise traditionalist state of the eighteenth and nineteenth centuries into feverish modernization in the realms of industry, communication, technology, and administration. Listless and incompetent native businessmen were forced to streamline, to rationalize, to expand, and to take risks. When this did not do, the state imported on a large scale foreign businessmen, foreign technicians, and foreign funds. Most recently this role of the state has been illustrated in the post-World War II efforts of the new nation-states of Asia.

Much more neglected has been the role of another element in modern history. This comprises the professions, the highly trained modern experts in medicine, law, engineering, education, science, and economics. In line with the West's absorption with the role of the businessman in shaping the modern world, the professions have often been dismissed as an automatic and marginal by-product of industrial society. Yet in countries like Russia, where the businessman was deficient as a Marxian "prime mover," the professions were a compensating element of major importance.

As a rule, the basic traits of modern society are identified with the businessman. But Bazarov and the novel "sons" of the sixties suggest that the functions of the professions in modern society produce in the professional man the same traits. This has also been the argument of Talcott Parsons' essay on "The Professions and Social Structure," which stresses the "rationality, functional specificity, and universalism" of the professions. If this is so, if the professions within themselves nurture the same key characteristics of modern industrial society as does the business entrepreneur, then the role of the latter need not be quite so crucial, quite so indispensable as Marxists and many non-Marxists have contended. In those societies where the business entrepreneur does not develop to his full-blown "ideal type," the professions, together with the state, may compensate for this historical deviation.

In the case of Russia, it was the state that, in the second half of the nineteenth century, first created the need for a professional middle class, through its economic and administrative modernization in the Great Reforms and its neomercantilist program for rapid industrialization. Then, and only then, did careers open by the thousands for law-

yers, economists, doctors, teachers, agronomers, engineers.*
In turn, this new professional middle class played as crucial
a role in Russian liberalism as the business middle class
did in parts of the West.

There is a basic difference, however, alongside this often
overlooked similarity. While the similarity is that of a mod-
ernization-oriented class, the difference concerns the concrete impact on society. Business reaches far deeper by
altering production and consumption than the professions
by providing new knowledge and new technical services.
This is particularly true when such modernization takes
place gradually and at the "grass roots," as Thorstein Veblen
emphasized in *Imperial Germany and the Industrial Revolution*. Probably in one case alone can the professions parallel
the role ascribed to business in Western history: a government that has both the desire and the ability to *force* modernization through a "revolution from above." Although attention has centered on the West's mass revolutions from
below, the opposite type has been at least as numerous and
important. In our own time such revolutions from above
tend to be accomplished by the professions themselves,
through a ruling "new class" of their own as in the USSR.
In earlier times, however, as in Imperial Russia, they served
as the junior partner of a pre-modern government attempt-

* Russia's first population census, in 1897, placed almost half a million
people in categories associated with the professions. The figure is not
satisfactory, however: on the one hand, some of these categories include
others outside the professions such as nurses and zemstvo clerks; on the
other hand, key professional people like lawyers not in private practice,
economists, and engineers are not shown apart from broader nonprofessional
categories. But inexact as the half-million figure is, it dramatizes the fact
that, by the end of the nineteenth century, Russia's professional middle
class was immeasurably greater than it had been in the time of either the
"fathers" or the "sons." These statistics can be found in *Obshchii svod po
imperii rezultatov razrabotki dannykh pervoi vseobshchei perepisi naseleniia*,
II, 296.

ing partial modernization to maintain power. It is in the latter role, and through concommitant political opposition, that a professional middle class like Russia's could up to a point substitute for the West's much emphasized "bourgeoisie." In contrasting ways, this began already with the "fathers" and the "sons."

From the "fathers" of the intelligentsia, the generation of the forties, the plebeian "sons" had taken over much of the missionary zeal, the sense of alienation from Russian life, the compulsion somehow to catapult their homeland out of its material and spiritual morass. But if the earlier generation partook of the nobility's creature comforts and social privileges, the "sons" of the sixties and seventies suffered all the hardships of the aspiring pariah in a nobility-dominated society. The "fathers," largely nobles, managed to oscillate between the otherworldliness of German metaphysics and French utopianism on the one hand and the "small deeds" liberalism of the Russian gentry on the other. The "sons" like Bazarov did not. As upstarts, as outsiders, they plunged instead into earnest, ostentatiously rude nihilist opposition to conventions in life and the arts, and into an equally earnest pursuit of scientific principles and formulas. If they considered politics at all, the "sons" (unlike the "fathers") were firmly committed to sweeping varieties of socialism, although theory still predominated over action. Thus to Bazarov's science, self-improvement, and nihilism, the other literary prototype of the "sons" — the more political hero of Nikolai Chernyshevski's *What Is to Be Done?* — added a hazy vision of socialist utopia and of revolutionary action. Most "sons" angrily attacked and suspected liberalism as a self-centered class movement of the nobility.

But as the "sons" were replaced by the "grandsons," by

the first full-blown generation of Russia's new professional middle class, the attitude toward liberalism did begin to change.

To be sure, the politically active segment of the intelligentsia continued to be — by age and temperament — more of a student movement than a political party; youthful ardor rather than brilliance or professional distinction still characterized the lower intelligentsia's political spokesmen. And the Russia of the "grandsons" was only relatively less backward and traditionalist than that of the "sons." Nonetheless, by the end of the nineteenth century a transformation had taken place with the Great Reforms and the dramatic industrialization that followed. Within the all-embracing government administration and especially its reformed branches like the judiciary, within modern-minded industry and zemstvo, in the provinces as well as in the mushrooming cities, a multitude of career opportunities and emotionally not unsatisfying jobs were open to the "grandsons." This was a decisive transformation indeed from the privations and frustrations of the "sons," which had fostered their gloomy conviction that their homeland had no berth for the intelligentsia, the true elite. Gone were the early intelligentsia's feebleness and isolation, gone too were some of the fire and puritanism. Gone as well was the initial dismay of the "fathers" at the parvenu coarseness of the "sons."

All this was paralleled by a changing usage of that most confusing term, "intelligentsia." A truly Russian invention, it was first applied to the "sons" of the 1860's. The term then signified an isolated, small, and classless missionary order of educated, theory-oriented men — men dedicated to Russia's material and spiritual salvation. The original emphasis was therefore on world view, on frame of mind, on outlook. But in Russia, as elsewhere, usage changed with the times. The country's partial modernization began a shift of emphasis from alienation to participation, and hence from the outsider's total ideology to the insider's more concrete concerns. Thus the "grandsons" altered the meaning of the term from outlook to occupation, and by the 1890's the term "intelligentsia" embraced all of the professions.* At the turn of the century, then, the terms "intelligentsia" and "professional middle class" became synonymous, and both equally applicable to the lower and upper intelligentsia.

Only after this vast transformation of the intelligentsia could the "grandsons" reconsider, slowly and gingerly, the fervent antiliberalism of the "sons." Only then did the new professional middle class begin to substitute for Russia's old but underdeveloped business middle class.

II

Whereas the gentry concentrated its activities in the zemstvo, the professions developed a variety of additional arenas for their cryptopolitics. Most potent among these were the universities. To be sure, Russian liberalism at the turn of the century was no more dominated by academe than was the "professorial" Frankfurt Parliament of 1848. But the articulateness and public eminence of professors in Russia, as in some other preindustrial societies, placed them in a strategic position. And most liberal currents enabled

---

* In the USSR, the scope of the term "intelligentsia" has expanded still further. To the professions were added the administrative middle class of white-collar workers, *Beamte, fonctionnaires.* It is noteworthy that in the United States today, on the contrary, "intelligentsia" (like "intellectual") approximates the initial Russian usage: a usually "left" minority engaged in literary and academic pursuits and preoccupied with general ideals and ideas on society.

them to remain within the confines of legal activity, which was important because, as in most continental universities, those in Russia were government financed and government controlled. As Russian liberalism broadened from its gentry base, professors were among the earliest and most prominent adherents from the professions.

The universities substituted in yet another way for proscribed political activities. By expanding tremendously after the middle of the century to accommodate the boom in professional training, they naturally became the first and usually the decisive political stimulant for future members of the professions. In these universities the earliest intelligentsia founded its philosophical circles in the 1830's, and from there populists in the 1870's and Marxists in the 1890's went straight into revolutionary work among the lower classes. Usually, however, student politics meant neither theoretical disputes nor revolutionary agitation, but something between the two. Such political activity most frequently took the form of student disorders: abstention from classes, public rallies, noisy street demonstrations. The immense impact of this species of politics in illiberal societies is still illustrated in Latin America and the Arab world — and more recently in the October Revolution of Poland and Hungary. In Russia it produced a similarly electrifying effect on the still somnolent political life of the 1890's.

The following causes or occasions for student disorders were enumerated at the time by a faculty commission of the University of Moscow:

[1] dissatisfaction with a [university disciplinary] inspector or some professors,

[2] memorial service for a popular writer [1890 and 1891],

[3] memorial service for the victims of the Khodynka misfortune of 1895 [during the Moscow coronation of Nicholas II],

[4] disorders occurring in other universities, as was the case in 1899 [St. Petersburg] and in the current year [1901, Kiev].[1]

Tracing student disorders back to the 1850's, the professors' report noted that since 1887 they had become almost annual at the University of Moscow. This upward trend of student disorders was confirmed by statistics on expulsions from the university, which had doubled in the six years from 1894 to 1899, as compared to the preceding seven years. During the later period, a total of 1214 students were expelled from the University of Moscow; two thirds of them were ousted by the university administration, and almost one third were arrested and exiled by the police.[2]

Whether student disorders were wholly nonpolitical or only externally so, the effect of expulsion was unmistakable. V. K. Plehve — in the 1880's a Deputy Minister of Education and later renowned as the hated pre-1905 Minister of the Interior — plaintively spelled out the consequences:

For the young people excluded from academic institutions, their lives turn out to be broken up at the very outset. Faced with inactivity, need, and deprivation, they become embittered against the whole social and political order. Those who previously merely leaned toward the seditious teachings now become completely indoctrinated by them. Those who are subjected to administrative exile begin even at the place of exile to exercise a bad influence on the local population. And if upon return they succeed in penetrating once again into institutions of higher learning, they become active agents of secret societies, and their attitude affects their friends. It corrupts them mentally and incites them to all kinds of disorder.[3]

The Deputy Minister of Education goes on to emphasize that student disorders bred the future participants of revolutionary terror. Yet this was not their only consequence. The fact is that these same university perturbations aroused and activated a majority of the professions that embraced liberalism rather than either socialism or revolutionary terror.

A graphic illustration of this comes from the memoirs of Vasili Maklakov, subsequently a leading trial lawyer and the Kadets' golden-tongued orator in the post-1905 Duma. Maklakov's family background had been conservative. Yet in 1887, his freshman year at the University of Moscow, much in Maklakov's life changed when a student struck an unpopular government inspector during a student performance attended by the tsar:

For the first time in my life I had seen a person who was sacrificing his whole life for something. Involuntarily there passed through my mind my mother's stories about saints who live in this world and what we read about "martyrs" who did not want to renounce their faith. I felt that I was seeing such a "martyr" with my own eyes. It was one of those impressions which in youth do not pass without an impact, although the consequences sometimes varied. This dim emotion possessed not only me apparently. Everyone wanted to do something, to manifest themselves somehow, but did not know what precisely they should do. An age-old tradition helped out.[4]

This age-old tradition was the resort to student disorders. Maklakov became one of Russia's most vocal antirevolutionary liberals, and his first student rally was emphatically apolitical. But it did start him on a career as student spokesman and organizer, of which his later liberal activism was a direct outgrowth.

Again and again in the decade before the 1905 Revolution, at moments when the government was unprepared or unconfident, and the lower classes as usual quiescent, such public manifestations of university students became inflated into national cataclysms. Although student unrests were often locally caused and profoundly nonpolitical, university students identified themselves completely with the professions for which they were heading. Thus they provided the professions, Russia's partial substitute for a business middle class, with an important mass base and striking force all its own. This challenges the commonplace that in modern western history only the concentrated urban lower classes, mainly the factory workers, have the numbers and the hardiness to stand up physically to government force. Nineteenth-century Russia, like other countries today, suggests that university students can rival "the masses." Their youthfulness, their close group contacts, their idealism and intellectuality — all these make university students at times even more effective.

Alongside the universities — and a daily press expanding rapidly since the middle of the century — the professions acquired another arena for their public manifestations. This consisted of a variety of professional and semiprofessional associations. However innocuous their titles or activities might sound, it was in such organizations more than anywhere else that the focal intelligentsia of Moscow and St. Petersburg congregated and interacted during the 1890's.

The occasion may have been an anniversary or memorial banquet, a periodic congress, an annual business meeting, a learned lecture, or the report of some obscure subcommission. But no matter what the occasion, the intelligentsia's revival after the oppressive eighties owed much to this new organizational arena in Moscow and St. Petersburg.

Perhaps the most distinguished of these professional associations was the Pirogov Society of Russian Doctors, founded in 1885. Less eminent but more politically oriented was the Moscow Society of Jurisprudence. Established in 1863 as an affiliate of the University of Moscow, it enjoyed considerable autonomy in pursuing its twofold interest in the law and broader political and economic problems. One of its special contributions to the professions was the organization in 1882 of a statistical section, which soon became the center for statisticians and economists throughout the country. Just how successful the Moscow Society of Jurisprudence was as a haven for the intelligentsia may be seen from the fact that in 1899 it was closed on government orders.

A similar fate awaited the oldest learned society in Russia, the Imperial Free Economic Society of St. Petersburg. Founded in 1765 under the sponsorship of Catherine II, it was granted almost complete autonomy — hence the "imperial" and the "free" in the title. In its original purpose it was similar to several dozen agricultural associations throughout the country, including the prominent Imperial Moscow Agricultural Society. All of them were intended to give the landowning nobility assistance on technical and economic questions in agriculture. During the 1890's, however, the Economic Society of St. Petersburg increasingly became a center for the professions rather than for gentleman-farmers. Here professors, agricultural experts, journalists, and leading exponents of feuding socialist camps argued rather freely on current economic issues and government policies.[5] Still more than the Moscow Society of Jurisprudence, the St. Petersburg Economic Society encountered suspicion and increasingly systematic opposition from the government. The climax of this opposition was reached in 1898, when the government insisted on revision of the society's ancient statutes. From 1900 on, the government paralyzed the numerous activities of the society by failing to approve its promptly submitted revisions.[6]

The Moscow Society of Jurisprudence was headed by a leading liberal: Sergei Muromtsev, the first president of the Duma. So was the Economic Society of St. Petersburg, whose president, Count Petr Geiden, belonged to the amorphous middle group in the liberal gentry. Himself a moderate constitutionalist, Geiden by his imposing bearing and skillful diplomacy helped the Economic Society to become the outstanding gathering place for the capital's less moderate intelligentsia. Hence the list of the society's approximately 800 members, and even more so of its officers, reads like a "Who's Who" of the professions' leading liberals and moderate socialists.[7] It is interesting to note that the Moscow Society of Jurisprudence correctly mirrored the predominance in the older capital of the gentry and moderate upper intelligentsia, whereas the Economic Society typified the greater role in St. Petersburg of the professions and of the more radical lower intelligentsia.

Journalists, writers, and literary specialists congregated in a hazy network of St. Petersburg writers' organizations. But hazy as they appeared, these organizations — notably the charitable Literary Fund, founded in 1859 — were quite effective, during moments of public stirring, in channeling the political action of the literati. Neither so hazy nor so lasting was the last type of organization that served as an arena for the professions: the committees on illiteracy of Moscow and of St. Petersburg. These groups provoked Lenin's jibe because toward the end of the 1880's they began to attract support from the lower intelligentsia (including Lenin's wife-to-be) as a small deeds means of educating "the people." Their network of adult education, of lecture classes, of elementary readings, and grammar textbooks reached into most provinces of Russia. The St. Petersburg Committee on Illiteracy was established in 1861, the year of the Emancipation Act, as a branch of the Economic Society. But its activities lagged until the 1880's when its membership spiraled from 127 to 1025.[8] The Moscow Committee on Illiteracy, a branch of the Imperial Moscow Society of Agriculture, likewise did not come to life until 1890. In both cities, the Committee on Illiteracy was akin to the university as a training ground for future liberal leaders. From the gentry and the professions alike came activists who at the first opportunity exchanged enlightenment for politics.

Given the fact that an autocracy's monopoly forces politically minded elements in the population to adopt substitutes, Russia's new professional middle class was doing rather well in the 1890's. It was not so much their existence itself that made these cryptopolitical and prepolitical arenas of the professions significant. Rather, it was the fact that the traditionalist, bureaucratized Russian monarchy lacked not only the apparatus but also the totalitarian aspirations to keep such organizations completely uncontroversial or loyal. To be sure, the government had its more ravenous officials and its periods of more intensive and more efficient thought control. But during the nineties the government never effectively checked the revival of public life. In this

context, between the protracted inertia of the 1880's and
the legalized political activity after 1905, the professional
and semiprofessional organizations became very important
as an invigorating new arena.

III

The only arena for the professions that outweighed these
professional associations was the zemstvo, the same network
of rural self-government that dominated the public life of
the gentry. The zemstvo did not monopolize the professions' activism and devotion as it did the liberal gentry's.
The upper intelligentsia remained primarily in numerous
courts, in private practice, in university teaching, and
in the government. Doctors, teachers, engineers likewise
centered their careers as much outside the zemstvo as in
it. But for much of the lower intelligentsia, it was the
zemstvo that provided the jobs. The growing complexity of
agriculture, together with the zemstvo's Kulturträger tasks,
resulted in an elaborate structure of administrative and
technical zemstvo personnel. More and more, this personnel
had to be drawn from the professions rather than from
either the dilettante gentry or the clerical white-collar
workers.

By the 1890's, the zemstvo thus employed thousands
upon thousands of doctors, teachers, agronomists, engineers,
botanists, veterinarians, economists, and the like. A peculiar
importance accrued to the statisticians, whose task was to
measure and record land and other property — a staggering
and technically crucial task indeed in the Russian countryside, where feudal and traditionalist relationships had pre-
vailed until so recently. The statisticians' special role was
further enhanced in 1895, when a government edict placed

on the zemstvos themselves the job of evaluating property and levying taxes on it to support their activities.

The zemstvo's professional personnel was universally referred to as "the third element," from a chance remark in 1899, when a Saratov vice-governor ranked it after the government (the zemstvo's first element) and the elective representatives (its second). By that date, this "third element" comprised no less than sixty-five or seventy thousand zemstvo employees.[9] And zemstvo service soon took on a political meaning for these professions as it had for the gentry. The more the other arenas were curbed by government restrictions, the more the zemstvo lured oppositionally inclined members of the professions. To them it became as much a cause, even a way of life, as it was for the liberal gentry. In turn the political orientation, or potential, of the zemstvo was immensely affected by the influx of the intelligentsia. The third element was not rooted in the nobility and was not so firmly linked to rural life and to the zemstvo. The mores and apprehensions that restrained the gentry and even its liberal contingent were largely alien to this lower intelligentsia. Hence in each zemstvo the third element became a democratizing lever exerting a leftward pull.

Nor was the influence of the third element confined to the zemstvo alone. When the government forbade national organizations of third element employees, this group spilled over into the existing professional organizations and soon dominated many of them. Thus within a decade of its founding in the mid-1880's, the Pirogov Society of Russian Doctors was under third element control. Likewise the large and active statistical section of the Moscow Society of Jurisprudence was dominated by this element, as was its successor, the statistical commission of the Economic Society in St. Petersburg. The third element, particularly its activist statisticians, thus provided much of the audience and much of the drive for the professional associations.

One other group felt the impact of the zemstvo third element. This was its employer, the gentry itself. The same factors that resulted in the rise of the professions — the Great Reforms, industrialization, the country's painful but steady drift away from feudal agriculture — also led to the economic decline of the gentry. A by-product of this decline was the wholesale entry of the younger gentry into the professions, of which by 1900 they made up a sizable minority. It is not surprising that sons of the liberal gentry, having joined the professions, would be particularly active in zemstvo work, either as paid employees in the third element or as landowner delegates in zemstvo assemblies.[10] These professionalized members of the gentry invariably acquired an outlook and even a social status distinct from the class of their origin. Their long and specialized training and their full-time occupations placed them in an impersonal, mobile, and urban atmosphere. This atmosphere was also more demanding and more absorbing than their family's pastoral gentleman-farmer style of life. And yet their whole upbringing, their continuing family ties, often also their continued ownership of land or estates — all this enabled them to influence the gentry as no outside group could.

The outcome was decisive for Russian liberalism. Inside the zemstvo it minimized distinctions between third element and gentry. And it prepared the liberal gentry to follow the intelligentsia leftward.

IV

If we ask, as we did about the gentry, what the professions' ideological trends were, we find two different answers by the 1890's. In the liberal direction, the ideology varied little from that of the liberal gentry, the distinction, if any, lying in the intelligentsia's relatively greater articulateness. For those further left, however, the nineties were a turning point — a period of massive ideological combats and re-alignments, resulting in a transformation within Russian socialism that affected liberalism profoundly.

Within the professions, the gentry's liberal slavophiles found few echoes. But much of the upper intelligentsia shared the views of the amorphous majority of gentry lib-erals. Leading jurists and leading professors, particularly, became the spokesmen for Russia's moderate liberals, con-stitutionalist but antiradical.

The embodiment of this moderate liberalism in the upper intelligentsia was Sergei Muromtsev. Born in the middle of the nineteenth century, a near-contemporary of Shipov and Petrunkevich, Muromtsev also came of a gentry family. He appeared to be an aloof, self-assured figure, whose assets were a precise, logical jurist's mind and an imposing presence rather than the moral zeal of Shipov or the combative defiance of Petrunkevich. Muromtsev was early drawn to academic pursuits, and during the 1870's — his greatest decade — he became law professor at the Uni-versity of Moscow and at the same time was increasingly active in the Moscow Society of Jurisprudence. This double role appealed to Muromtsev because his ideal was to serve both learning and public life: "After my professorial work, my activity in editing the journal [of the Society of Juris-prudence] is of foremost importance, because it is to serve as the means of influencing the public outside the univer-sity." [11]

Muromtsev's outspoken opposition to the government's control of the university, however, led to his dismissal from the University of Moscow during the archconservatives' ascendancy in the early 1880's. He continued to write in the general press — notably a series of "letters from Moscow," in 1885 as in 1880[12] — and he also became active as a delegate to zemstvo and duma assemblies. But by then his major scholarly works were behind him, and his dream of combining scholarship with public activity gave way to routine, though much respected, legal work. Muromtsev did not re-emerge as a leading public figure until the 1905 Revolution, when his mixture of outspoken constitutionalism with moderation and a solemn bearing won him election as president of the first Duma.

Characteristic of Russia's moderate liberals was Muromtsev's lifelong worship of the Great Reforms of the 1860's. From them he drew and nourished his faith in future political reforms, which in turn were the focus of his legal thinking and his writing. His conception of the Great Reforms was reiterated in 1880:

> The question arises in general: which of the currents now openly fighting will win out in the near future? Will victory remain on the side of the destroyers who, hidden behind the name of "protectors" (*okhraniteli*), are undermining the best ideas of the 1860's? Or will it be achieved by the opposite side, the side of the genuine protectors and conservatives who stand for the preservation of these ideas? [13]

In the same year, Muromtsev wrote a memorandum that still throws more light than any other source on the position of Russia's moderate liberals. Muromtsev was aided in writing this document by two other nationally known Moscow liberals — Aleksandr Chuprov, professor of economics at the University of Moscow, and Vasili Skalon, pioneering board chairman of the Moscow district zemstvo;[14] like Koshelev, both of these men were perennial publicists and zemstvo activists, and both were editors and copublishers of *Russkie vedomosti*. The resulting document was signed by twenty-five prominent Moscow professors, lawyers, and other professional men, and was submitted to General Loris-Melikov, the reform minister of Alexander II's last days.

Despite the special tone of moderation traditionally used in addressing a high official, the 1880 memorandum revealed its liberal spirit in answering its own opening question: "How can the evil [of revolutionary terrorism] be remedied?"

First. That the principal reason for the morbid form which the contest with the Government has taken is the absence in Russia of any opportunity for the free development of public opinion and the free exercise of public activity.

Second. That the evil cannot be eradicated by any sort of repressive measures.

Third. That the present condition of the people, many of whose most urgent needs are wholly unsatisfied, constitutes ample cause for dissatisfaction, and that this dissatisfaction, having no means of free expression, necessarily manifests itself in morbid forms.

Fourth. That the causes which underlie this widespread discontent cannot be removed by government action alone, but require the friendly cooperation of all the vital forces of society.

The memorandum reached a climax with an enumeration of the major ills besetting Russia:

First. The first and most important of society's unsatisfied demands is the demand for an opportunity to act. . . . The Russian people are becoming more and more impressed with the conviction that an empire so extensive and a social life so complicated as ours cannot be managed exclusively by *chinovniki* [officials]. . . .

Second. Another demand of society which at the present time is even less satisfied than the desire for political activity is the demand for personal security. The indispensable conditions upon which the very existence of modern society depends are free courts, freedom from arrest and search with proper precautions and safeguards, responsibility of officials for illegal detention and imprisonment, and the due observance of all the legal formalities of public and controversial [sic] trial in cases involving the infliction of punishment. . . .

Third. There is in the present condition of the courts and of local self-government another cause of irritation, arising out of the Government itself. . . .

Fourth. That which happened to representative institutions and to the courts happened also to the press, and in perhaps an even worse form.

The specific political recommendations of the memorandum are equally revealing:

The only way to extricate the country from its present position is to summon an independent [assembly] consisting of representatives of the zemstvos; to give that [assembly] a share in the control of national life; and to securely guarantee personal rights, freedom of thought, and freedom of speech.[15]

The 1880 memorandum represented a detailed and fervent recapitulation of classical Western liberalism, with its stress on the individual and on individual liberties, with its faith in education, in rationalism, reasonableness, and harmony, in the primacy of political reforms and constitutions. The memorandum omitted social and economic questions, however, and made no mention of political democracy or universal suffrage. It suggested the convening of estates-general consisting of zemstvo delegates, rather than a popularly elected constituent assembly. These characteristics, along with their strong condemnation of revolutionaries, distinguished Muromtsev and his moderate current from other liberals in the intelligentsia. In his demands Muromtsev was closer to the slavophile Shipov and the *Rechtsstaat* liberal Chicherin than to the gentry constitutionalist Petrunkevich.

V

Petrunkevich's counterpart in the intelligentsia was Pavel Miliukov, destined to succeed him in 1905 as the leader of Russian liberalism. Before abandoning himself to politics, before becoming the foremost oppositional leader in Russia's parliamentary experiment from 1905 to 1917, Miliukov lived through a different career: when still in his thirties, he became the most prominent and widely read Russian historian between the time of his own teacher, the great Vasili Kliuchevski, and the Soviet era.

Miliukov was born in Moscow in 1859 — a decade or more after Shipov, Petrunkevich, and Muromtsev — the

son of a successful but often impecunious architect and a
temperamental, domineering noblewoman. Even in his high
school days one of Miliukov's lasting traits appeared: his
development was shaped by voracious reading and his
private theoretical enthusiasms. Even when he became a
skillful writer and speaker, awesome cerebration took the
place of charm or warmth. Hence he clearly preferred the
impersonal, formalized activities of parliament and legal
political parties after 1905 to the amorphous and twilight
nature of the earlier oppositional sects. Whereas Muromtsev
reveled in his role as consummately skillful parliamentarian,
Miliukov's cool passion found its métier in the tactical and
programmatic maneuvering of a parliamentary party.

At the University of Moscow Miliukov participated in
student activities, Russia's earliest form of political schooling, and even then he was committed to the nonsocialist
groupings. After Alexander II's assassination in 1881, he
was expelled for these activities, but he returned soon and
decided on an academic career, settling eventually on
Russian history. From the mid-1880's on, Miliukov taught
for a decade at the University of Moscow as *Privatdozent*.
The following decade, lasting to the height of the 1905 Revolution, he spent in travel, mostly involuntary. Accused of
antigovernmental activities and sentiments, Miliukov was
twice imprisoned briefly and was banished several times
from Moscow and then St. Petersburg. On some occasions
exile took him to provincial towns in Russia, on others
abroad. Thus he participated in archeological excavations
in Greece, explored Russian history in the British Museum,
was engaged as a history professor at the University of
Sofia, became a specialist in Balkan history and politics, and
visited the United States several times to lecture (in Eng-

lish) at the University of Chicago and the Lowell Institute in Boston.

Yet it was during these two decades before the 1905 Revolution that Miliukov began and completed all of the scholarly works that earned him the status of Russia's leading historian after Kliuchevski. Two monographs focused on the economic and social history of Russia, one during Peter the Great's reforms and the other during the Muscovite period. In two other volumes Miliukov turned to intellectual history, dealing first with Russian historiography to the 1830's and then with the early development of the Russian intelligentsia. Miliukov's last scholarly work turned out to be his magnum opus and a continuing best seller in pre-1917 Russia. This was his three-volume synthesis of Russian culture, *Ocherki po istorii russkoi kultury*. With his characteristically encyclopedic approach, Miliukov's description of "culture" included detailed analyses of ethnography, archeology, social structure, economic history, political thought and institutions, as well as the history of literature, art, education, the church, philosophy, and science.

Late in life, Miliukov himself offered a clue to the roots of his philosophy of history and his ideology:

I succeeded in remaining independent of the influence of both main currents ruling over the minds of the Russian intelligentsia of the last quarter of the nineteenth century, populism and Marxism. This I owe before all else to circumstances beyond my control: that I belong to the generation that is younger than the generation of the seventies which was enthusiastic about populism, but older than the generation of the eighties and nineties, which pledged allegiance to Marx. . . . Instead, I experienced as early as my student years the impact of the two founders of contemporary sociology — the creator of positivist philosophy, Auguste Comte, and the author of synthetic philosophy, Herbert Spencer. . . .[16]

Although Miliukov grew up in a lower intelligentsia dominated by socialism, he himself was thus most influenced by nonsocialist, largely liberal ideas from the West: the rationalism and scientism of Comte, of Spencer, and of another of his Western favorites, John Stuart Mill. This combination explains his Petrunkevich-like broadening of liberalism to add social reforms and political democracy to Muromtsev's traditional liberal demands. It also explains why Miliukov did not become an active ally of gentry liberalism until the eve of the 1905 Revolution. Instead, polemicizing in the 1890's with populists and with Marxists about his magnum opus, he confessed to a partial sympathy for both: theoretically for Marxism — for its economic materialism and westernism if not its monism — and personally as much for populists as for liberals. Like Petrunkevich — and very much unlike Muromtsev, Chicherin, or Shipov — Miliukov is thus a new type of liberal of the late nineteenth century, an *homme du gauche* best typified by Clemenceau and his Radicals.

Until the turn of the century, neither Miliukov's personal circumstances nor the nature of Russian oppositional currents favored his emergence as liberal leader of the intelligentsia. For until then he was not active politically or as a publicist, and except for a stint as Moscow leader of the mass education movement of the 1890's, he confined himself mainly to scholarly writing and teaching. But even in these fields Miliukov, combining liberal individualism and rationalism with a new emphasis on democracy, affirmed the decisive role of the masses:

> How far mankind will travel on this path we do not know. But there is only one path by which the spontaneous historical process can be supplanted by the conscious: the gradual replacement of socially expedient acts of individuals by the socially expedient behavior of the masses.[17]

Along with his complete commitment to democracy and social reform, Miliukov reasserted the Russian liberals' traditional westernism, their opposition to the slavophile contention that Russia must follow a unique path. Following European liberalism, as well as the teachings of Comte and Spencer, Miliukov argued that all societies were subject, despite local variations, to the same laws of evolution. He linked the agrarian socialists' populism to slavophile doctrines and declared "democratic liberalism of the newest type" [18] to be the heir of the westernizers among the early intelligentsia.* This "democratic liberalism of the newest type" was the ideology that Miliukov espoused from the outset. Yet until the twentieth century neither he nor others in this current of intelligentsia liberalism worked out any detailed statement of their views.

* This is one of the few instances when Russian liberals employed "liberalism" as a self-description. From the middle of the nineteenth century on, the right in Russia equated liberalism with utopianism and disguised radicalism; the left associated it with ineffectuality and narrow class interest. In response, liberals shifted to another term: "the public" (*obshchestvo*). Also widespread were the cognate "public opinion" and "the movement of public opinion" (the best rendition, in this context, of *obshchestvennoe dvizhenie*). By the turn of the twentieth century, the more militant term "liberation movement" gained in favor. Both "the public" and "liberation movement" were on occasion appropriated by distinctly antiliberal radicals. But even in the radical usage these terms implied at least participation by liberals and partly liberal slogans and methods.

VI

The nineties were marked by two upswings in public life akin to the movements of the late 1870's. The first revival came with the great famine of 1891–1892. The government sought first to minimize its importance and later to channel all famine relief through its own officials. But as the famine spread, so did public excitement and the conviction that the government could not and would not handle famine relief properly. An appeal by Leo Tolstoy touched off a wave of activism in the gentry and the intelligentsia, aimed at direct aid to the starving rural areas. Thus, for the first time, the old socialist dreams of "going to the people" coalesced in practice with the ideals of small deeds liberalism. Similarly, the zemstvo notables and third element joined in action with the intelligentsia's growing professional organizations. The St. Petersburg and Moscow committees on illiteracy in particular became the headquarters for relief activities where many a future liberal leader got his start. This unforeseen and exhilarating thaw after the freeze of the 1880's touched off the regrouping and crystallization of the opposition that marked all of the nineties. New contacts, new ideas, new self-confidence were gained by the intelligentsia, the zemstvo, the liberals. But neither in organization nor in program did Russian liberalism continue to reflect this heroic brief interlude, and soon public political life seemed to recede into its old narrow framework.

The second public upswing of the nineties came with the death of Alexander III in 1894. His son and heir, Nicholas II, was young and little known, and high hopes of his reign spread across the land. These hopes were particularly strong in the gentry; hence the customary zemstvo messages to the new monarch adopted an accommodating and optimistic

tone. One of the few messages to voice an unmistakably oppositional view came once again from the zemstvo of Tver,
the old constitutionalist stronghold. But by then a new
leader had replaced the Bakunin group of the Great Reforms and the 1879 resolution, a young disciple of theirs and
of Petrunkevich. This was Fedor Rodichev, who — like another liberal, Maklakov — became after 1905 one of the great
orators of the Duma. A contemporary of Miliukov born in
Tver, Rodichev from the outset devoted himself to gentle-
man-farming and to the zemstvo there. At first he embraced
the slavophile and populist idealization of the peasant commune, but by 1881 contact with the peasantry had converted him from Romantic communalism to the liberal
emphasis on individual freedom. The young Rodichev submitted through the Tver zemstvo an outspoken memorandum urging that the peasants be assured equal legal rights
with others, freed of excessive financial burdens, and encouraged to become individual landowners.[19]

Two years before the accession of Nicholas II Rodichev
had been elected chairman of the Tver province zemstvo's
executive board, but the appointment was not confirmed by
the government. Nevertheless Rodichev obtained the Tver
zemstvo's approval of his own constitutionalist message to
the new tsar. Initially approved by the zemstvo assembly
in the form of a telegram to Nicholas II, the address had to
be reconsidered when the government insisted on its being
signed by all participants and then transmitted through the
Ministry of the Interior. Despite apprehensions and de-
fections caused by the government action, a majority of 33
delegates signed the address.

Beginning with the habitual pledges of loyalty and devotion to monarch and monarchy, the Tver address of 1894
reiterated familiar liberal hopes of reform from above:

We trust that our happiness will increase and grow firmer under an unflinching adherence to the laws on the part both of the people and of the authorities; for the laws, which in Russia embody the expression of the Sovereign's will, must be placed above the accidental intentions of individual representatives of the Government. We ardently believe that the rights of individuals and of public institutions will be steadfastly safeguarded.

We look forward, Sire, to its being possible and rightful for public institutions to express their views on matters concerning them, so that an expression of the requirements and thought of representatives of the Russian people, and not only of the administration, may reach the heights of the throne. . . .[20]

This Tver address caused a sensation. So did the government's reaction: the removal of Rodichev from the chairmanship of the Tver zemstvo deputation to the tsar's reception of 17 January 1895. At this reception the young and hardly known Nicholas II uttered his historic condemnation of the Tver address and of "senseless dreams." To the assembled representatives of the zemstvo, the nobility, and the city dumas, the tsar made an ominous speech:

I am glad to see representatives of all classes assembled to declare their loyal sentiments. I believe in the sincerity of those sentiments, which have ever been proper to every Russian. But I am aware that of late, in some zemstvo assemblies, [there] have been heard voices of persons who have been carried away by senseless dreams of the participation of zemstvo representatives in the affairs of internal administration. Let it be known to all that I, while devoting all my energies to the good of the people, shall maintain the principle of autocracy just as firmly and unflinchingly as did my unforgettable father.[21]

The Tver address of 1894 had voiced the opposition's modest hopes, hopes couched in language far more veiled and mild than the Tver resolution of 1879 or the Muromtsev memorandum of 1880. But it is characteristic of this small deeds phase of Russian liberalism, its defensive stance and lack of militancy, that the young tsar's chilling rebuke was met largely by disenchantment which was as inaudible as it was deep. To be sure, Rodichev published abroad an anonymous pamphlet in which he analyzed and condemned the tsar's speech. But the conclusion of this pamphlet hardly went beyond the minimal liberal demands of the Tver address.[22]

Another similar pamphlet also appeared abroad in 1895. Its author, Prince Dmitri Shakhovskoi, belonged to Rodichev's generation of younger gentry constitutionalists but was as gentle as Rodichev was ardent. Shakhovskoi had evolved from an agrarian socialist with Tolstoyan leanings into one of the leaders of pre-1905 Russian liberalism. He started his public career as a third element employee of the Tver zemstvo and then became a landowner delegate to the zemstvo assembly of his own nearby province. His pseudonymous pamphlet of 1895 was more critical than Rodichev's of zemstvo apathy and gentry conservatism, and it also reiterated Petrunkevich's old emphasis on the need for social reforms and a constituent assembly.[23] In general, the Shakhovskoi pamphlet adhered far more than Rodichev's to the "democratic liberalism" of Petrunkevich and Miliukov. It reflected the thinking of a whole new circle formed by Moscow constitutionalists around the again active Petrunkevich, a group to which Shakhovskoi as well as Rodichev belonged.

Both pamphlets went unnoticed, however. And after the great famine had stimulated a clandestine constitutionalist conference in 1892 and again in 1893, the Petrunkevich circle could neither convene another nor succeed in publishing a periodical abroad. Four soon-forgotten pamphlets were the only direct outcome for the constitutionalists of the upswings of 1891 and 1894. Although Rodichev was deprived of his political rights and a few other Tver leaders were reprimanded or punished, none even suffered banishment as did Petrunkevich in 1879.

VII

If severe reprisals do not account for Russian liberalism's lack of vitality and resilience after both upswings in the 1890's, how then can we explain it? One explanation goes beyond the confines of Russia. It is no accident that Russian liberalism did not readily become dynamic or militant in the later nineteenth century. For throughout Europe the period had passed when liberalism was the new revolutionary creed. The eighteenth century had reflected the comparative simplicity of its own society by an individualistic, laissez faire ideology. In the Enlightenment, in the great French Revolution, among England's Philosophical Radicals, and even in the 1848 revolutions this faith, though changing, still persisted. But meanwhile new victories and new defeats were altering the picture. The lower classes could no longer be expected either to be passive or to follow the liberal banner. The liberal triumphs had stimulated a vigorous restoration on the right, a more democratic radicalism and socialism on the left, and all around the novel passions of romanticism and nationalism. Meanwhile industrialization, urbanization, and other modern institutions were complicating society to an extent that made liberals pause, whether or not they had achieved power.

In the second half of the nineteenth century, the result for liberalism was not a total defeat or a total disappearance. On the contrary, in terms of political institutions and even the mores of daily life, the secular, individualistic, and rationalist principles of liberalism were advancing in much of the world. But the old zeal, the old confidence were gone, and liberalism in theory and in practice increasingly became a static rather than a revolutionary force. Victorian England offers examples of this, as do the Rechtsstaat liberals of Bismarck Germany and the French liberals before Clemenceau. Such a slowing down, such a cooling of ardor is not unique to liberalism. In our time socialism — the very doctrine that replaced liberalism in the revolutionary vanguard of Western ideology — has undergone very much the same process of deceleration and deflation. Both movements lost momentum as some of their major goals were attained — and as new problems arose that the founders did not and could not foresee. It is this kind of liberalism, then, still important but far less vital than before, that we encounter in the Russia of the 1890's, as we did in the earlier small deeds phase of gentry liberalism.

A second explanation of the nonmilitancy of Russian liberalism can be found inside Russia, where the nineties in many ways resembled the decades after the early 1860's. The state, despite occasional wavering and ministerial changes, continued to exercise a monopoly over politics as well as power. Its two lapses in control — during the famines of 1891 and 1892 and again during the imperial succession in 1894 and 1895 — were briefer than the previous one, which had lasted four years, from the Balkan war of 1877–78 until the assassination of Alexander II. Furthermore, in the 1890's the government made no gestures or concessions to liberal opinion as it had during 1877–1881. This governmental policy, in turn, assured passivity in the gentry, because much of the gentry became liberal only when government benevolence or government concessions seemed likely.

The fact that the gentry continued in the 1890's to be the leading liberal element, with the professions only an important new potential, explains much of the small deeds timidity and nonmilitancy. And since a still-passive population unavoidably focused short-run liberal hopes on the government itself, the liberal tone most acceptable to the government — and most plausible for the liberals themselves — was one of loyalty and accommodation. This is borne out by the major gathering of gentry leaders after the Tver address and the tsar's frigid response. In December 1895, the Imperial Moscow Society of Agriculture convened the Sixth All-Russian Congress of Landowners. It is characteristic that the chairman of this large congress was Shipov, the least militant of liberal zemstvo leaders, and that its lengthy resolutions centered on technical agricultural problems and on the government — government support, government approval, and government participation in the proposed undertakings.[24]

Shakhovskoi, the conscientious chronicler of constitutionalist endeavors, has written a revealing reminiscence of the congress and of the role of its constitutionalist minority:

all questions of a political nature were systematically avoided. A considerable number of zemstvo men ap-

peared at the session. As I have mentioned, there had
been no advance agreement by the zemstvo men of the
more left current. Shipov probably took steps to attract
to the congress the more active zemstvo men he knew.
At the congress, however, two groups could be clearly
distinguished. A central group, purely technically oriented, was headed by Shipov and prominently represented by Nikolai Khomiakov [like Shipov a slavophile
liberal]. A group of zemstvo men further left attempted
to base the deliberations more on principle and to inject
some political themes. These themes could be reduced
to two points: representation for the zemstvo in central
[state] organs and the formation [on the peasants' canton
level] of the "small zemstvo unit." . . .

Among the participants in the [congress' zemstvo]
session were not a few future [constitutionalist] leaders
of zemstvo congresses and members of the First State
Duma. . . . But their speeches were distinctly not of a
programmatic nature and at times were reduced to nothing
by the insistent efforts of the central group.[25]

Even this narrowly technical, conciliatory attempt was
followed by government rebuke. When Shipov, as chairman of the Moscow zemstvo board, sought together with
other zemstvo officials to arrange a joint zemstvo offering
in honor of the monarch's coronation in Moscow, this meeting was forbidden.[26] After initially being refused, the chairmen of province zemstvo boards were allowed to convene
privately during the Nizhnii Novgorod fair of 1896, and
nineteen out of thirty-five did meet to take up technical
zemstvo problems. But a similar meeting for the following
year was prohibited.[27] Thus the last conference led by

Shipov for some time occurred during the 1898 unveiling of a Moscow statue for Alexander II, the monarch of the Great Reforms. In speeches at a private gathering zemstvo leaders contrasted the Great Reforms glowingly with their own time,[28] but they did not even discuss resuming national conferences of zemstvo officials; instead they merely voted a plaque to Alexander II. In another abortive effort, a zemstvo periodical that was contemplated as a substitute for the proscribed national conferences failed through government vetoes and zemstvo apathy.

If continuing liberal weakness in the first half of the 1890's is explainable externally by the sagging momentum of European liberalism and internally by the strength of the state and the nobility's economic and political dependence on it — if this be true, did nothing change from the 1870's and 1880's? Was small deeds liberalism of the gentry as dominant in the early 1890's as it had been earlier?

In terms of appearances as well as activities, the picture had changed little. The gentry still represented the bulk of Russian liberals, and the liberal gentry's tactics and activities continued to stress Kulturtäger small deeds downward and equally nonpolitical and local accommodation upward. Yet, aided by hindsight, we can perceive in the first half of the 1890's a major change in Russian liberalism: its substratum and its potentials. For the intelligentsia, the young professional middle class, had at last found ample and meaningful employment; it also now developed a growing network of professional organizations that encouraged contacts and *esprit de corps*, if not yet political action. The ideological mellowing that could be expected to accompany this group's rise in social and economic position had not manifested itself in the early 1890's. But at that time there were two harbingers of the change.

First, despite its purist and socialist sympathies of earlier days the lower intelligentsia entered into close collaboration with liberal gentry on a professional basis. This was true above all in the zemstvo, where the new and ever-expanding staff of third element professional employees was bound to seek and find support among liberal zemstvo leaders. At the same time Russian liberals began changing, too. The third element, with its outspokenly socialist and democratic sympathies, had an inestimable impact on gentry liberals in every zemstvo. The recent flow of younger noblemen into the professions reinforced this current of new and left ideas. And the constitutionalist grouping in Russian liberalism gained new leaders. Some of these — notably Miliukov — came from the lower intelligentsia, and some, like Rodichev and Shakhovskoi, were gentry activists younger than Petrunkevich. The constitutionalists were still a minority. Their unbelligerent gentry audience forced them to sound in public more like the moderate Muromtsev or Shipov or Chicherin than like their own ideals and clandestine utterances. Yet the constitutionalists' slow growth inside the intelligentsia and elsewhere was important; this was the liberal current furthest left, and hence closest to the intelligentsia's radical traditions.

The new intelligentsia, the nascent professional middle class, was potentially a peculiar substitute for Russia's underdeveloped business middle class. Its plebeian "sons," however, opposed Russian liberalism vehemently in the 1860's and 1870's because their life-situation differed starkly from that of the gentry. These "sons," like their rebellious and zealous embodiments in the heroes of Turgenev's *Fathers and Sons* and Chernyshevski's *What Is to Be Done?* could hardly embrace the tepid liberalism of small deeds. With the 1890's, however, the changes in both the gentry and the intelligentsia encouraged numerous professional and organizational contacts. In the realm of ideology — and of politics in general — such a *rapprochement* between the lower intelligentsia and the liberal gentry was yet to come.

Chapter Three

THIRD FORCE

The people do not give a damn for your landowners' constitution.

Mikhailovski to Petrunkevich, 1878

I am not afraid to be a lone wolf and to take what I need from Kant and Fichte and Marx and Brentano and Rodbertus and Böhm-Bawerk and Lassalle.

Struve in 1901

Since the "grandsons" neither were nor felt as alienated or superfluous as the "sons," the lower intelligentsia's transformation was bound to cause an ideological mellowing. But when this ideological change did come, in the 1890's, it was not as profound as the change in status. In addition to the usual time lag between new status and new ideology, Russia's young professional middle class still felt its own power to be very limited and shaky. Hence it was far more political, and politically oppositional, than were the professions of more advanced and prosperous societies. The mellowing was also counteracted by the lower intelligentsia's radical traditions. This led to ideological ambivalence: most of the prospering lower intelligentsia shared the new, less intransigent, more gradualist views; yet they continued to aid and admire revolutionary sects and, in the tradition of the "sons," to prefer socialism over liberalism. Thousands unaffiliated with the tiny socialist sects agreed with those true believers that the promised land was a new socialist society, and revolution the only path to salvation. Not before the 1890's did socialists within the intelligentsia begin themselves to deviate in large numbers. Signs of ideological disaffection appeared first in the older agrarian socialism of the early nineties. Only afterwards, in the second half of the decade, did the young Marxist movement succumb to a similar malady.

To Russian liberalism, this process of deviation among socialists was as decisive ideologically as the emergence of a large professional middle class had been sociologically. As a result, for the first time the lower intelligentsia became a third force between revolutionary socialism and liberalism.*

I

As a movement, socialism has drawn its support from two elements. One component is the lower classes, urban and rural. The objectives of this labor component as a rule were short-run: less arduous and more secure employment. It is the other component of socialism, the lower intelligentsia, that adds the grand sweep, the idiom, and the blueprint of a wholly new and wondrous society.

In *A Theory of the Labor Movement*, Selig Perlman has emphasized that intellectuals in socialist movements share a common conception of labor. It is an essentially mystical conception of an abstract "mass" in the grip of an abstract "force." But Perlman's work also suggests how greatly the relationship between the intellectual and the labor movement has varied from country to country, from period to period. In the United States labor did not welcome the intellectual, nor was it friendly to socialism. In England

* Lately, several American studies have dealt with the subject of this chapter: Haimson, *The Russian Marxists and the Origins of Bolshevism*, Treadgold, *Lenin and his Rivals*, Hammond, *Lenin on Trade Unions and Revolutions*, Billington, *Mikhailovsky and Russian Populism*, and Mendel's Harvard dissertation on "Legal Populism and Legal Marxism." But they approached the subject in terms of socialism rather than liberalism, and did not emphasize the 1890's as a turning point in the lower intelligentsia's attitude toward liberalism. The same is true of a recent difference in interpretation between two other American historians: von Laue, "Legal Marxism and the Fate of Capitalism in Russia" in the January 1956 *Review of Politics*, and Baron's rejoinder, of the same title, in the *American Slavic and East European Review* of April 1957.

the two groups collaborated more harmoniously than elsewhere. In Germany the intellectual declined from leader
to subordinate. Only in Russia did the intellectual retain
free sway.

Russia's uniqueness in this realm was the outgrowth of
one main factor: unlike its counterparts in America, England, and Germany, socialism in Russia lacked not only an
internal but also an external check on the intellectual.
Farther west, a more or less liberal society enabled socialism's laboring element to express itself, to counterbalance
the intellectual through self-governing trade-unions, co-
operatives, and fraternal orders. At the same time, Western
societies tended to soften and domesticate socialist movements through parliamentary concessions and ameliorations
in lower-class existence. But in Russia, due to government
policy as well as the population's backwardness and conservatism, the socialist movement lacked a labor element
altogether and the intellectual was left to his own devices.*
Outside the movement, too, neither parliamentary politics
nor the chores of mass organizations existed to blunt or
satiate the intellectual's political appetites. It is profoundly
ironic that in nineteenth-century Russia — as in eighteenth-
century France — a devoutly autocratic government re-
leased rather than impeded the flights of fancy, the dreams
of millennial utopias so appealing to intellectuals of all

* The gulf between intelligentsia and lower classes is stressed likewise
in the major new work on Russian socialism, Radkey's *The Peasant Foes
of Bolshevism*: "When all is said and done, Populism was, in essence, a
movement composed of intellectuals who championed the cause of the
peasantry, and Marxism, a movement composed of intellectuals who championed the cause of the proletariat . . . the impartial observer knows that
the intelligentsia thoroughly dominated both socialist movements and that
neither the peasants nor the workers were masters in what was supposed to
be their own house." Radkey, however, appears to ascribe this situation
to intellectuals alone rather than to an underdeveloped society as a whole,
including "the people."

times. In both countries, autocracy did this by isolating the intellectual from the hurly-burly of practical politics and from the pressures for compromise inherent in larger and more heterogeneous groups. As a result, Russia's socialists were — in frame of mind and mode of life — rather like political émigés in a foreign country. Both were expatriates living outside of the thick mesh of society's customs and restraints. Many of the foremost Russian socialists — Herzen and Bakunin, Lavrov, Kropotkin and Tkachev, the Marxists from Plekhanov to Trotsky — actually were émigés most of their adult life, thus adding the expatriate's physical displacement to the political vacuum created by autocracy.

The socialist leaders and sects, of course, committed themselves more continuously and more absolutely to this way of life than did the rest of the lower intelligentsia. But the group as a whole no less than the dedicated sects shared the traumas and dreams of their forerunners: extreme alienation, extreme isolation, extreme "maximalist" intransigence. This tradition as much as liberal meekness explains why liberalism was inevitably scorned, why for several decades the socialists insisted on "going it alone" even when advocating liberal measures. It is this tradition that in the 1890's began, but only began, to be questioned among the socialist faithful themselves.

II

Of Russia's socialist currents in the nineties, populism had an older history than Marxism and its "legal" and "economist" deviations. The term "populism" has a multitude of definitions, some conflicting and some overlapping. The broadest general meaning is "love of the people," the ever idealized peasant bulk of the population. This broad formulation of populism breaks down into various strands: the cultural populism of enlightening the people and exploring their folk culture; the philosophical populism of theories of history, culture, and society built around the people; and finally the political populism of blueprints for future political systems, as well as action by or for the people. To the lower intelligentsia, populism usually meant socialism, an agrarian socialism centered on Russia's peasant commune. In part influenced by the slavophiles, the populist intelligentsia for half a century idealized the commune as the unique path to a total social transformation, to a non-Western, essentially pastoral and anarchist society. Bypassing political reforms, such a transformation would come about either through a sweeping peasant upheaval or through a coup by revolutionary intellectuals.

Not before the 1890's did a populist group appear that consciously and most influentially attacked the peasant commune as a living model for Russian socialism and instead urged collaboration with liberalism. This group did not abandon agrarian socialism, but it chose political reform over antireform upheaval, and "legal" as against clandestine populism. These choices explain the group's willingness to modify the intelligentsia's tradition of antiliberalism. Its acceptance of political action meant that it was not wholly skeptical, as other populists remained, about achieving government reforms except through revolution and terror. Its "legal" — nonclandestine — form meant that instead of functioning underground like revolutionary conspiracies it would operate above the surface of Russian public life, and hence it could collaborate with traditionally anticonspiratorial liberals. And its loss of faith in the commune made it more eager to support, or to use, other political and social forces than the once idealized peasantry.

External influences furthered this *rapprochement*. The 1880's had decimated revolutionary populism. The growth of Russian capitalism had begun to expose the fragility of the peasant commune, while the famine of 1891 revealed that the peasant was as unprepared to embrace the revolutionary gospel then as he had been almost two decades before, in the 1874 movement of "going to the people." Meanwhile, the liberal gentry was welcoming Kulturträger populism and the intelligentsia third element into the zemstvo, and the new constitutionalism of Petrunkevich and Miliukov was making liberalism ideologically less suspect. Equally important for the populists, still emphatically agrarian, was the fact that in Russia a gentry-rooted liberalism had never "debased" itself by speaking for the business middle class. Ever since the Romantic reaction to industrialism, *épater le bourgeois* had been a lasting fixation and favorite pursuit of both landed conservatives and radical intellectuals. In Russia, unlike the West, the liberals could participate in anathematizing "the bourgeoisie." In the striking words of Russia's foremost liberal journal of the time, *Vestnik Evropy:* "Our liberals are least of all inclined to adhere to the principle 'laisser faire, laisser passer' in any of the areas of state or popular life . . . since we do not have a bourgeoisie in the Western European sense of the word, we also do not have a bourgeois liberalism." [1]

The two mentors and symbols of the new proliberal populism were among the most revered and most discussed figures in Russia's lower intelligentsia of the 1890's. One was the veteran literary critic and theorist, Nikolai Mikhailovski. The younger of the two was Vladimir Korolenko, a popular novelist.

Mikhailovski, like Petrunkevich, was born into the gentry in the early 1840's. By the 1870's he had become a universally read editor of the leading populist review, *Otechest-vennye zapiski*. From then on, he poured forth a stream of essays, reviews, and books. Published legally under the censorship in Russia, the writings of Mikhailovski dealt with philosophy, literature, aesthetics. As Russia's leading Comtian positivist and "subjective" sociologist, he exalted the individual, the hero, the intelligentsia. But, inferentially at least, all of his writings revolved around politics and socialism.

It is characteristic of Mikhailovski's "legal populism" that it did not keep him from aiding the clandestine revolutionary operations of the terrorist organization *Narodnaia volia*. He participated in the writing of its 1879 program, which paralleled Petrunkevich's pamphlet of the same year by centering its demands on a constituent assembly. But if for Petrunkevich this was a maximum program, for the revolutionary intellectuals in Narodnaia volia it was merely a minimum program: "This [constituent assembly] is of course far from an ideal form of manifesting the popular will, but in practice it is the only one feasible at the moment. . . ." [2] And when Petrunkevich a few months earlier had sought to enlist Mikhailovski's collaboration with liberals in the gentry, he received a brusque refusal climaxed by the previously quoted assurance that "the people do not give a damn for your landowners' constitution." [3] Mikhailovski remained true to Narodnaia volia's formula for a constituent assembly as a minimum program, but by the 1890's circumstances had made him more amenable to collaboration with liberals.

From 1891 on, the populist journal *Russkoe bogatstvo* was the arena for Mikhailovski and his followers. Korolenko, the most prominent of these, became its literary editor. About ten years younger than Mikhailovski, Korolenko re-

peatedly expressed the deepest admiration for the older
man. As early as 1890 he wrote Mikhailovski that "for a
magazine in which you were to be editor I would turn my-
self inside out." Two years later he described himself as one
of Mikhailovski's "friends, partisans, and — of course —
pupils." Korolenko warmly supported Mikhailovski's populism in its opposition both to the quietism and neoslavophilism of other populists and to the Marxist emphasis on
proletarian hegemony over "the aggregate of all the laboring classes."[4] To Maksim Gorki, his protégé and friend,
Korolenko reiterated the faith that he shared with Mikhailovski in the need for "many a decade" of patient legal
work and small deeds, before "the sick but strong tooth"
of autocracy could be pulled out.[5]

Although Mikhailovski and Korolenko were the two outstanding personalities on *Russkoe bogatstvo*, three of its
other editors later helped advance the collaboration with
liberals. Mikhailovski and Korolenko foreshadowed this
changed attitude in their writings, but the other editors
actually sponsored and led organizations jointly with
liberals from the gentry and intelligentsia.

The oldest of these pro-liberal editors was Nikolai Annenski. A contemporary of Mikhailovski — with whom he
served on the staff of *Otechestvennye zapiski* — and an
intimate friend of Korolenko, Annenski was active as an
economist and journalist. But, above all, he was the country's foremost zemstvo statistician; and statisticians, in turn,
were politically the most activist group in the zemstvo's
third element. After thirteen years of government service,
mainly as a statistician, Annenski was banished for revolutionary activity. Following his exile, he served for four
years as head of the statistical department of the Kazan
zemstvo, and for eight years more he held the same post

in the Nizhnii Novgorod zemstvo. From then until 1900, he combined writing and editorial work on *Russkoe bogatstvo* with his duties as head of the statistical section of the St. Petersburg municipal duma.

The second pro-liberal editor of *Russkoe bogatstvo* was Aleksei Peshekhonov. Born in 1867, he was twenty-five years younger than both Mikhailovski and Annenski. Like the latter he served as the head of a zemstvo's statistical department (in Poltava); Peshekhonov, too, had been exiled and wrote a great deal for *Russkoe bogatstvo*. The third editor was Benedikt Miakotin, a contemporary of Peshekhonov, and the only professional historian in the group. Miakotin's prolonged archival explorations into the social history of the Ukraine delayed his joining the *Russkoe bogatstvo* group until the late nineties. It was Miakotin who first introduced to this circle his fellow historian Miliukov, who found it personally rather compatible in the 1890's.

Through Mikhailovski and Peshekhonov, the *Russkoe bogatstvo* group became associated, loosely but definitely, with another pro-liberal populist venture. This was the founding in 1893 of the People's Rights (*Narodnoe pravo*) Party. Stimulated by the intelligentsia's stirring, both during and after the 1891 famine, populists multiplied their attempts to unify their decimated and scattered adherents into a new organization. In the case of the People's Rights Party, a few months after its founding almost all of the members — as well as the clandestine printing equipment — were seized in one police raid. The People's Rights Party differed from similarly brief and ill-fated attempts at populist unification in two respects: in its programmatic moderation and its repeated emphasis on collaboration with liberals and liberal causes.

Although the People's Rights Party espoused agrarian socialism, it believed neither in revolutionary organizations nor in revolutionary work in the villages. Instead, the emphasis was on action by "public opinion." In the Russian parlance of the day, this meant the opinion of politically-minded — and nonrevolutionary — segments of the nobility and the intelligentsia. The People's Rights program is a complete if hazy reflection of this attitude. Like the party's title, the program assigned priority to achieving political freedom. It emphasized the government's mistreatment of the zemstvo. And it stated that the distinctly unrevolutionary aim of the People's Rights Party was "to unite all oppositional elements of the country and to organize an active force which, with the help of all moral and spiritual forces at its command, will vanquish autocracy and guarantee to each the rights of citizens and men." [6]

The short-lived People's Rights Party is forgotten today. If Mikhailovski and his *Russkoe bogatstvo* group are still remembered, it is not as a pro-liberal deviation from revolutionary socialism but as the earliest polemical target of Russian Marxism. Mikhailovski drew the heaviest fire — not as the most orthodox among populists, but as the most prominent and respected. The half-heartedness of his rejoinders, indecisive even if often stinging, was elucidated with feeling in a later letter by Korolenko:

A certain misunderstanding has occurred about this term "populism." This current was once simply generally democratic, and it began when the industrial elements were indeed very weak. A split in this faction started long before [organized Russian] Marxism. Mikhailovski was the first to circulate Marx's ideas and to defend them in Russian journals. And he was also the first to argue against the schemes of V. V. [Vorontsov]. When a tendency emerged in populism . . . pointing toward a unique form of quietism and neoslavophilism, Mikhailovski sharply rose up against it. But at this time, Marxism, young and fervent, proclaimed that Russia was exclusively an industrial country and that the entire peasantry was passive material, material for mechanical reshaping in the inevitable process of proletarianization. At that point Mikhailovski dropped the polemic against "right" populism and turned to the other front. And his opponents assumed that by fighting Mikhailovski they were fighting populism. Mikhailovski did not object, since to a certain extent the word expressed the essence of the argument: the interests of the *people* as an aggregate of all the laboring classes on the one hand, the interests of the industrial proletariat alone on the other.[7]

In terms of populism's attitude to Russian liberalism, the interest of this polemic lies not in its substance but in its revelation of Mikhailovski's steady departure from orthodoxy. His readiness to collaborate with liberals, and the even greater readiness of his associates on *Russkoe bogatstvo*, grew out of their abandonment of revolutionary orthodoxy and messianic faith: Mikhailovski's mellowing, his withdrawal from orthodoxy in his fifties, meant a conscious new skepticism and flexibility. As he wrote in 1895 in a personal letter, "I think that in the near future the sun will not shine. In general it may light up or not light up. In the natural course of events itself I see no guarantee."[8]

In the case of *Russkoe bogatstvo's* legal populism, then, deviations from the revolutionary tradition reflected growing unorthodoxy of views about both the peasantry's potential and the liberals' potential. But this did not mean that the legal populists had abandoned socialism or even collaboration with conspiratorial revolutionary ventures. Indeed, Peshekhonov testified that "Miakotin and I, although we did not belong formally to the S. R. [Socialist Revolutionary] Party, were close to it almost from its inception. Not leaving the open arena, which was for us the most important, we likewise participated in the conspiratorial activity of the party." [9] Nonetheless, socialist and even pro-revolutionary as the *Russkoe bogatstvo* group remained, its emphasis was now more than ever on the "open arena," on nonrevolutionary political action by intelligentsia and gentry, liberal no less than socialist.

III

If the earliest deviation from revolutionary socialism may be labeled "legal populism," the second is generally known as "legal Marxism." Usually two different usages of this latter term are confused. In the broadest sense "legal Marxism" is a technical term, referring to the practice of the Marxists in the 1890's of publishing their writings inside Russia legally. This procedure was followed by Georgi Plekhanov, the founder of Russian Marxism, by Lenin, and by the future Menshevik, Aleksandr Potresov; but it was followed equally by those who, narrowly and substantively speaking, were *the* legal Marxists. Their insistence on legality went beyond a tactic for reaching a broader audience and eventually embraced basic problems of ideology and politics. Only this latter group — a loose handful of young Russian writers in the 1890's — deviated, like the populists, from orthodoxy and from revolutionary socialism.

When Russian Marxism, both legal and orthodox, voiced the fervent battle cry of the new generation of the nineties, populism appeared to be nearing its demise. The populist tradition had survived the organizational disasters and intellectual torpor of the eighties, but not the sweeping industrialization of the next decade. Industrialization brought with it Russia's first impressive concentrations of factory workers as well as a visible decline in the peasant commune. At the same time, the intelligentsia's own transformation into a modern, science-minded professional middle class made populism seem too old-fashioned, too sentimental, and too unscientific for many. Yet the Marxist triumph was far from absolute. After 1900 a new populism, organizationally unified and ideologically streamlined, recaptured support in the lower intelligentsia through the appeal of non-Marxian terror and of Viktor Chernov's theoretical prowess. And the Marxist triumph itself was followed by two internal crises, crises in which revolutionary orthodoxy was opposed, for a time successfully. The first such opposition came from the legal Marxists, the second from the "economists" who followed the legal Marxist deviation chronologically but not ideologically.

The legal Marxists' ability to oppose the orthodox revolutionaries successfully was due to their prominence in the initial Marxist engagement with the populists. In that confrontation, the legal Marxists rather than the revolutionaries wrote the most, were read the most, and appeared most freely and frequently in the influential St. Petersburg debates. In retrospect, the picture has been altered by the Bolshevik victory, the mountainous republications of orthodox writings and correspondence, and the outside world's avid interest in the origins of Bolshevism. Now it is the orthodox Marxists, and above all the determined young Lenin, who appear to have led the troops and won the battle. At the time, in the second half of the 1890's, the older Marxists around Plekhanov had already spent a decade in far-off Switzerland, while the younger generation — the future Bolshevik and Menshevik leaders — were in exile or were absorbed in conspiratorial organizing among factory workers. Write and polemicize they also did, but it was the legal Marxists who at the time achieved the greatest prominence as slayers of the populist dragon.*

Among the handful of legal Marxists, two figures stand out: Berdiaev and Struve. Nikolai Berdiaev, born in 1874 — only two decades before the great populist-Marxist combat — came of an aristocratic and prosperous family in the south of Russia. While a student at the University of Kiev, he became active in the local Social Democratic circle, and in 1898 he was banished for three years to a small northern town in European Russia. During this exile he started writing and composed his first book. The dominant strain

---

* The literary outpourings of the legal Marxists appeared in a succession of periodicals (*Novoe slovo* in 1897, *Nachalo* in 1899, *Zhizn* from 1899 to 1901, to a lesser extent *Mir bozhii* and *Nauchnoe obrazovanie*) and also in a number of widely read and much disputed works on philosophy and economics. The earliest of these works appeared in 1894, when Peter Struve came out with his famous polemic against populism (*Kriticheskie zametki k voprosu ob ekonomicheskom razvitii Rossii*), and Mikhail Tugan-Baranovski published a study of economic crises in England (*Promyshlennye krizisy v sovremennoi Anglii*). A second major work by Tugan-Baranovski, a classic on the history of Russian industry, appeared in 1898 (*Russkaia fabrika v proshlom i v nastoiashchem*). The next year Struve published a long key essay on Marxist theory, which did not appear in book form until 1905 (*Marksovaia teoriia sotsialnogo razvitiia*). In 1900 came Sergei Bulgakov's two-volume work on capitalism and agriculture (*Kapitalizm i zemledelie*). The same year Nikolai Berdiaev issued a philosophical critique of Mikhailovski (and of orthodox Marxism) with a lengthy preface by Struve on the subject (*Subektivizm i individualizm v obshchestvennoi filosofii*). This was followed by several collections of essays: in 1902 Struve's *Na raznye temy* and the collective *Problemy idealizma*, in 1903 Bulgakov's *Ot marksizma k idealizmu*, in 1906 Berdiaev's *Sub specie aeternitatis*. In 1903 Tugan-Baranovski surveyed economic thought (*Ocherki po noveishei istorii politicheskoi ekonomii*), and in 1905 Marxist theory (*Teoreticheskie osnovy marksizma*).

in Berdiaev's thought was mysticism; indeed after 1917, as an émigré in Paris, he became one of the world's most noted and prolific Christian mystics. As a youth sickly, introspective, and intensely anti-"bourgeois," Berdiaev in his autobiography identified himself with "aristocratic radicalism" and termed himself "a Russian romantic of the early twentieth century." [10]

If Berdiaev is of interest because of his later eminence in the West, Struve stood out at the time as the best-known and the most active of the legal Marxists. He remained a stormy petrel in Russia's political and intellectual life until the 1917 Revolution forced him to endure the gray frustrations of emigration. In the opening years of the twentieth century Struve became one of the leading figures of Russian liberalism. Hence his early development and his metamorphosis from Marxism are of special interest.

Struve was born in 1870, the son of a St. Petersburg government official who had been rapidly promoted and then prematurely forced to retire for his nonradical but oppositional notions. From the outset, Struve strikingly manifested the intellectual and political precociousness typical of nineteenth-century Russia, a precociousness shared by two others also born in 1870: the leaders of Menshevism and Bolshevism, Julius Martov and Lenin. At the University of St. Petersburg, Struve was a student leader, participated in clandestine Social Democratic agitation among workers, and was briefly arrested and later placed under police surveillance. But even at that time and increasingly from then on, Struve's Marxism characteristically took a public and literary rather than conspiratorial form.

By his early twenties Struve had developed a sparkling, lightly combative style combined with a Miliukov-like erudition and an exceptionally prolific output. In the decade preceding his formal espousal of Russian liberalism in 1902, Struve published more than a hundred theoretical articles on economics, technical, philosophy, esthetics, sociology, history, current events, and ideology. They appeared in Russian learned reviews, in the theoretical organs of the German Social Democrats, in widely read St. Petersburg newspapers and magazines, and in Russia's leading encyclopedia.

His basic trait, a "lone wolf" unorthodoxy, appeared early. While Struve was still at the university, a fellow student said of him: "Can't understand him. Is he a German Social Democrat, or is he a liberal from *Vestnik Evropy?*" [11] This question was a shrewd and valid one. For the theoretical and organizational grandeur of Germany's Social Democratic Party awed and attracted Struve as Russia's sect-like revolutionary Marxism did not. Nor did he ever break completely with the gentry liberalism represented by the journal *Vestnik Evropy.* Thus Struve's personal friends of the mid-1890's included the staunchly liberal Rodichev and Shakhovskoi no less than the future Menshevik leader Potresov, "my closest fellow-thinker." [12] This duality was also borne out by Struve's two major ventures in the mid-nineties. In 1894 he published a strongly Marxist book against populism, a best seller and the first such attack to appear inside Russia. The next year, after the tsar's rebuke to the Tver zemstvo, he wrote and circulated a liberal "Open Letter to Nicholas II." In moderate language he chided, but did not condemn, the zemstvo for the mildness of its addresses to the tsar, to whom he promised a "peaceful but steady and conscious struggle for the necessary elbow-room [for political activity]." [13]

How can we explain this ideological ambivalence in the

young Struve? Struve's earliest ideological development is still little known except through his own later and incomplete memoirs. In them he recalled that "in my childhood I had patriotic, nationalistic impulses, tinged with dynastic and at the same time Slavophil sympathies, verging on hatred for the revolutionary movement." But in his teens he was increasingly drawn to the antislavophile westernism of the liberal *Vestnik Evropy.* "Soon 'love of freedom' was born in my heart with something like an elemental force when I was fifteen. . . . I was thus a constitutionalist and a political liberal before the problem of Socialism arose before my mind." Struve's memoirs offer a revealing reconstruction of his conversion to Marxism:

Just as naturally as in 1885 I had become, by passion and by conviction, a liberal and a constitutionalist, so about three years later I became, but this time *by conviction* only, a Social Democrat. By conviction only; for Socialism, however it be understood, never inspired any *emotions* in me, still less a passion. It was simply by way of reasoning that I became an adept of Socialism, having come to the conclusion that it was a historically inevitable result of the objective process of economic development.[14]

During a journey abroad in 1890, Struve was "carried away by German Social Democracy and its successes." At the same time, the liberal, antirevolutionary writings of Turgenev and Dragomanov moved him deeply. In retrospect, Struve thus pictured the appeal of Marxism to his generation as a means only, as an anxiously craved assurance that Russia would be modernized, and therefore free.

In the 1890's most of Struve's writings stressed two attitudes. One was a sharp attack on the populists and their hopes of bypassing capitalism, and industrialization, through the peasant commune. The second was a warm endorsement of Marx's theories and his superior school of "scientific socialism." These two themes dominated Struve's first book in 1894. But alongside antipopulism and Marxism a third theme also appeared in the 1894 book, and within a few years Struve cited this theme in claiming priority as a revisionist of Marxism:

> Mr. Mikhailovski asserts that the critical trend in Russian Marxism is mainly a reflection of a turn which took place in the West European literature of Marxism. But this is factually incorrect. Of what did the most characteristic features of the critical [revisionist] trend in Marxism consist? The attempts to combine Marxism with the critical philosophy originating in Kant, and with the denial of the concepts known as *Zusammenbruchstheorie* and *Verelendungstheorie*. Finally it meant an extremely cautious attitude toward the complicated and difficult problem of agrarian evolution. "Critical Observations" made the first attempt in Marxist literature to add critical philosophy [neo-Kantianism] to the development and grounding of Marxism. The book developed views containing in them the denial of the *Zusammenbruchstheorie* and the *Verelendungstheorie*. And lastly, in relation to agrarian evolution I recommended the essential caution and expressed views which had nothing in common with orthodoxy [and] which did not remain without influence on subsequent literature.[15]

As possible evidence for Struve's later claim of revisionist primacy, his book did announce at the outset that "adhering on some basic questions to an outlook clarified in [Western] literature, [the author] in no way considered himself tied by the letter and law of any doctrine. He was not infected with orthodoxy." On the philosophical aspects of Marxism, Struve specified that

> we cannot but admit that the *purely philosophical basis* of [historical materialism] has not been created, and that it has not yet mastered that vast concrete material which universal history represents. What is required, apparently, is a *review of facts* from the point of view of the new theory; what is required is the *criticism of the theory* with facts.

Elsewhere in the book he noted that, while Marxism predicted a catastrophic collapse of capitalism, it was at the same time fighting for gradual ameliorations. Finally, with few of the qualifications customary for Marxists, Struve devoted much of the book to welcoming capitalism to Russia, ending with the much quoted phrase: "Let us admit our lack of culture and undergo the capitalist schooling." [16]

Struve's "revisionism" in 1894 was, however, adumbrated rather than articulated, general attitude and passing remarks taking the place of explicit formulations. That Struve was not yet ready to break with the prevailing orthodoxy of Russian Marxism is confirmed by his close collaboration with it throughout the second half of the nineties. In 1895, for example, he contributed an essay to a short-lived volume among whose contributors orthodox Marxists predominated.[17] Later, during an official trip for the Social Democratic movement, Struve served as a member of the Russian delegation at the London congress of the Socialist International and delivered a report there.[18] He had also established contact with the German party and with the émigré leaders of Russian revolutionary Marxism, and he wrote two revealing and militantly Social Democratic articles on the Russian strikes. One of these articles appeared in a leading German Social Democratic journal, the other in the émigré organ of Russian Social Democrats. Here Struve argued that unfortunately Russian liberals had failed to move on from their traditional cultural emphasis to the necessary political militancy, and hence Russia's Social Democrats were obliged to lead not only the working class but also the liberals. The goal throughout, he declared, should be political liberty, and at the moment only Russian workers and a Social Democratic movement could provide the lead. "Helping the workers' cause in one way or another, any Russian person will advance the great national cause of winning political liberties." [19]

Struve's best-remembered collaboration with the orthodox Marxists came in 1898. The scattered Social Democratic groups in Russia and abroad had decided to hold a congress to create a unified party. They selected Struve to write the official manifesto for the new party, which its ill-fated first congress approved with few amendments. Later Struve emphasized that the manifesto, "drafted by me, still expressed the official or orthodox conception. I did my best to avoid putting into it my own views." [20] But more significant is the fact that Struve was willing to write it at all, and that the Social Democratic groups had asked him to do so and that when he had written it they accepted it with few changes. Moreover, Struve could readily subscribe to the frequently cited key passage:

> The farther to the east in Europe, the more politically weak, cowardly, and base the bourgeoisie becomes, and

the greater the cultural and political tasks of the proletariat. On its strong shoulders the Russian working class
must and will carry the cause of winning political
liberties.[21]

Struve's authorship of the official party proclamation
marks the climax of his collaboration with orthodox Marxism. The following year, in 1899, Struve published two
lengthy essays in which, as he wrote soon after, "the new
world view of the author is formulated." [22] Although in the
intervening years Struve had continued to voice the kind
of revisionist and even liberal views that characterized
Kriticheskie zametki in 1894, it was only in 1899 that his
position emerged clearly. A year before, Eduard Bernstein
had published his dramatic and detailed pleas for a revision
of Marxism. This suggests that Bernstein's writings and
the resulting polemic did stimulate Struve to crystallize his
own "revisionism" as he had never done before.

One of Struve's new essays — "Die Marxsche Theorie der
sozialen Entwicklung" — appeared in a German socialist
journal, and was intended as a grand critique of Marxism.
Struve's main objection was to the utopianism of the dialectical approach to history. This approach, Struve insisted,
contradicts and invalidates historical materialism, the great
(and to him still correct) cornerstone of Marxism. In actual
life, the dialectical opposition between capitalism and socialism does not exist, but rather the latter grows gradually
out of the former. Thus the collapse of capitalism stressed
by orthodox Marxists would automatically bring with it a
paralled diminution of the likelihood of socialism. Likewise,
the identification of social revolution (in reality a gradual
process) with political revolution (a sudden seizure of
power) is wholly invalid. In no case could social revolution

either lead to or be brought on by what Struve termed the "jacobin-blanquist" concept of seizing power.

Despite the 1899 essays and increasing friction with the orthodox leaders of Russian Marxism, Struve's collaboration with them had not ceased. En route abroad from their places of banishment inside Russia, Lenin, Martov, and Potresov met Struve and Tugan-Baranovski in Pskov in the spring of 1900 to discuss the joint publication abroad of a periodical. A year later, after additional lengthy negotiations with these and the older émigré leaders in Munich, Struve cosigned a formal publishing agreement with Plekhanov.[23] For extraneous reasons the project failed to materialize. Yet *Iskra,* the new orthodox organ abroad, did publish Struve. It printed not only a lengthy article by him but also a Struve-edited pamphlet which contained a sensational secret memorandum by Minister of Finance Witte, "leaked" to Struve by a third party.[24]

The article that Struve published in *Iskra* played a major role in the final break. In it he wrote not as a revisionist Marxist — as he had in 1899 — but as a liberal. He now repeatedly and emphatically sided with the zemstvo, the liberal gentry, and gradualism; revolution and the revolutionary movement were condoned, but only as a means to liberal ends. After an extensive correspondence among the orthodox leaders they responded with a vehement attack by Lenin[25] on both Struve and gentry liberalism.*

---

* Lenin played a peculiar role in the relations of the orthodox to Struve. His reaction to Struve's early *Kriticheskie zametki* was a typically slashing book-length attack, by far the sharpest of the orthodox comments: *Ekonomicheskoe soderzhanie narodnichestva i kritika ego v knige g. Struve.* Thereafter, however, Lenin repeatedly urged organizational conciliation and was personally thrown into close contact with Struve. When Lenin was banished in 1897, it fell to Struve to obtain most of the many books that Lenin had had his family mail regularly and openly to Siberia. Struve also played a decisive role in getting legally published the two major works

Struve's "lone wolf" unorthodoxy, which had always irritated Lenin, remained a lifetime trait. But his early wavering between Marxism and liberalism — whether it had been only tactical (as he subsequently stated) or in part also ideological (as his contemporary actions and writings suggest) — had dissipated by the 1900's. Lenin's attack, together with the earlier failure to publish a joint organ, furthered Struve's drift away from the orthodox Marxists. More decisive, however, was the end of the Marxist-populist battle. This obviated the need for the erstwhile kind of ideological and organizational alliance that Struve later described:

> I understood then with my mind as well as my emotions, that first of all it was necessary to carry on and finish a united struggle against populism and prepare a new practical and viable conception of Russian reality. Never orthodox myself, in these two tasks I felt quite in solidarity with orthodoxy.[26]

Yet, although Struve and the other legal Marxists were unmistakably influenced by Bernstein and German revisionism, they never became Russian "Bernsteinians." For one thing, the legal Marxists had repeatedly expressed a low

that Lenin composed while in Siberia. One work was on the development of Russian capitalism (1898), most of which had originally appeared in the Struve-edited *Novoe slovo*. Finally, Struve provided Lenin and his wife with a publisher's contract to translate while in exile the large work of Sidney and Beatrice Webb, *Industrial Democracy*. All this was accompanied by frequent and friendly exchanges, to be found in Lenin's *Pisma k rodnym*. Lenin stated his reason for maintaining relations with the ideologically suspect Struve in an 1899 letter to Potresov: "in the present composition of our *Genossen* there are not a few *verkleideten Liberalen*. . . . This is, so to say, our fortune; this allows us to count on an easier and quicker beginning which requires precisely the utilization of all these *verkleideten*." (This letter is reproduced in Lenin, *Sochineniia*, 4th ed., XXXIV, 8–11.)

opinion of Bernstein's theoretical prowess. Thus Struve in
one of his few extant letters from this period wrote that
Berstein is "poor philosophically, somewhat philistine, and
theoretically reasons rather unclearly." [27] More fundamentally, the German revisionists failed to appeal uncondition-
ally because the legal Marxists were no longer interested
in the Social Democratic movement (or even in Marx),
while the Germans still were. Almost all of Struve's and
Berdiaev's revisionist polemics stressed not the problems of
socialism and labor but their own neo-Kantian philosophy.
Philosophical idealism, individualism, and eventually liberalism came to predominate more and more over the
negative slogans of antiorthodoxy and "critical" Marxism.
The German revisionists had long been members of their
Marxist party, and they remained members. The legal
Marxists, on the other hand, came to the Social Democratic
movement only during the populist battle. It was never a
marriage, and now the end of that affair meant the end of
the whole relationship. No wonder then that legal Marxism
denied formal ties with German revisionism.

After the populist battle the legal Marxists, a handful of
still youthful and influential men, were free to attack socialist ultraorthodoxy while themselves intoning the gentler
tunes of liberalism. Having championed Russian Marxism
during its heroic days, they — and above all Struve — could
be sure of a hearing from all of the intelligentsia, something
few nonsocialists could hope for.

IV

"Economism," a third deviation from orthodox revolutionary socialism, developed at the turn of the century. Unlike
the rather homogeneous legal populism and legal Marxism,

economism took three very different forms during its hey-day. Of these three forms, the two larger — we may label them the "tactical" and the "practical" — remained within the camp of revolutionary Marxism. Only the third and smallest — the "theoretical" — blossomed into a definite deviation. But for some time it overlapped organizationally and ideologically with the other two. And its writings continued to influence the other economists decisively even after the differences became uppermost.

Theoretical economism consisted not of a handful of people, as did legal Marxism, but merely of a man and his wife — Sergei Prokopovich and Ekaterina Kuskova. Both were from the gentry and were near-contemporaries of Struve, Lenin, and Martov — the 1870 vintage. Prokopo-vich and Kuskova were a close Russian counterpart to Sidney and Beatrice Webb. In each case the husband was a prolific scholar, somewhat awkward and stolid, the wife more agile and emotional. And in each case an unlikely combination led to half a century of intimate collaboration, although Russia had less use and glory for Prokopovich and Kuskova than Britain for the Webbs.

The Russian pair lived abroad between 1894 and 1898, first in Brussels and then in Berlin, while Prokopovich was working on an ambitious history of the European labor movement. It was there that the young couple reconsidered their earlier populist and later Marxist views. Prokopovich "lost a good half of them during the investigations [for the book]," as he states in the preface to its first volume.[28] In the spring of 1897 he first got in touch with the Social Democratic center in Switzerland, and, after almost a year of orthodoxy and then neutrality,[29] he issued strong objections against the orthodox elders. During the same year

Kuskova and Prokopovich returned to Russia, where their position was crystallized and formulated in writing.*

Why and how did theoretical economism differ from the other forms? Why did it and not the others represent a deviation, a departure from socialist orthodoxy? The answer is that the theoretical economists first combined the views of the other two forms, and then moved away from orthodoxy far beyond either.

Thus the theoretical economists praised the key "tactical" pamphlet of 1894, *Ob agitatsii.* They accepted the central doctrine of tactical economism: economic agitation and the resulting local action were at the moment — in the mid-1890's — the best tactic to further political goals. But unlike the tactical economists, Prokopovich and Kuskova did not stop there. For their views also embraced much of the practical economists' "pure trade-unionism" — the belief that the labor movement must be built on the substantive and organizational needs, not of the intellectuals, but of the workers themselves.[30] Again and again Kuskova and Prokopovich insisted that "the consciousness of the workers is not dough which 'we' [the intellectuals] are called upon to mold according to our own manner and image. 'We' and 'our' efforts can only supplement what life teaches the worker." [31]

---

* Compared to the writings of the legal Marxists, those of the theoretical economists were not only fewer but also less known. This is especially true of Kuskova's letters to "Timofei" Kopelzon, the foreign representative of the Jewish Social Democratic *Bund* and a leading tactical economist, as well as of her and her husband's lengthy exchanges with Plekhanov and other émigré orthodox leaders. Also devoted to theoretical economism are Prokopovich's first major works, on the labor movements of Germany and Belgium and on the theories of Marx. The best remembered statement of theoretical economism was Kuskova's brief and hastily composed "Credo" of 1899. This Credo has acquired historical durability by its complete incorporation that year into Lenin's sharply worded "Protest" against it, signed by seventeen Social Democratic exiles in Siberia.

Another facet of theoretical economism earned its authors the reputation of revisionists and led to their being labeled disciples of Bernstein. Kuskova did indeed write that "Marxism is not a dead doctrine, but a guiding theory which is developing and expanding. Criticism of Marxism, and also of the working out of several undeveloped questions, is quite important at the present moment." [32] And the concluding paragraph of Prokopovich's book on Marxist theory again echoed Bernstein: "In contrast to Marx, we expect future progress not from the worsening of the situation of the laboring classes, but from the rise of their economic welfare and the growth of their social influence." [33] Like Bernstein, the theoretical economists inveighed against dogmatism in orthodox Marxism. They condemned continuing talk of political and social revolution and rather saw socialism as liberalism's heir in the realm of evolutionary reforms. They believed that in their homeland, the workers' nonrevolutionary economic demands of the labor movement and the resulting government concessions "are preparing the ground for changing the entire state system of Russia." [34]

Yet Prokopovich and Kuskova went beyond Bernstein as they went beyond practical and tactical economism. Bernstein himself devoted a lengthy footnote in his main revisionist work to the dissent voiced by "a Russian socialist who stands very near to my views, S. Prokopovich." [35] The theoretical economists disagreed with Bernstein's retention of "science," of theory, in an important position for shaping the program of the Social Democratic movements; to them, theory was no more a guide for long-range party goals than for specific policies. Instead, the great ideological experience of their youth — their enthusiasm for Belgium and its labor movement — moved Prokopovich and Kuskova to champion two principles that in contemporary socialism are usually associated with the English Fabians. One is an antitheoretical empiricism. The other is the stress on the workers' "bread and butter" needs, reflected in their own functional organizations, particularly trade-unions and co-operatives, as opposed to the intellectuals' political predilections.

Theoretical economism was applied to Russian politics most clearly in Kuskova's renowned Credo of 1899.[36] Repudiated in print by proponents of the two other forms of economism, the Credo contained the theoretical economists' unique blend of tactical and practical economism, of Bernsteinian revisionism, and of ideas distilled from the Belgian labor movement. The Credo affirmed that political activity in Russia was out of the question:

> The talk about an independent workers' political party is nothing more or less than the product of the attempt to transplant alien tasks and alien results to our soil. At present, the Russian Marxist presents a sad spectacle. His practical tasks at the present time are paltry, his theoretical knowledge, insofar as he utilizes it, not as an instrument of research, but as a scheme for activity, is worthless for the purpose of fulfilling even these paltry practical tasks. Moreover, these borrowed schemes are harmful from the practical point of view.

This unmerciful portrait of the "paltry" sectarianism and dogmatism of Russian Marxism is followed by an equally unorthodox final prescription, a prescription that eventually brought Kuskova and Prokopovich close to Russian liberalism: "There is only one way out for the Russian Marxist: he must participate, i.e. assist, in the economic struggle of the proletariat, and take part in liberal oppositional activity."

V

The amorphous, scarcely articulated ideology of legal populism, the elaborate but as yet uncrystallized philosophical idealism of the legal Marxists, the simpler organizational emphasis of the theoretical economists — each represented a major and temporarily dominant inroad into the revolutionary orthodoxy of Russian socialism. Organizationally, orthodox populism and Marxism revived early in the twentieth century. But they did not and could not regain the monopoly their nineteenth-century forerunners had enjoyed so long. For the lower intelligentsia was in the throes of adjusting its ideology to its improved social and economic standing. Recurrent attacks on revolutionary orthodoxy had by that time resulted in a new flexibility, an ideological mellowing, which made possible collaboration with nonsocialists. What a change, indeed, between Mikhailovski's utter scorn of liberalism in the 1870's and Struve's unabashed pro-liberal heterodoxy two decades later.

That the intelligentsia's deviations from socialist orthodoxy were peculiarly Russian was illustrated ironically when Karl Kautsky, the orthodox theorist of German Marxism, wrote to the revisionist Berdiaev in 1899: "The Russians are destined to develop theoretical Marxism further. Thanks to absolutism the Russians have time for this. In Russia the social[ist] movement is still a struggle for knowledge and not for power." [37] The irony was that Russian autocracy and the resulting deformations in the intelligentsia did not encourage the greater depth, the greater insights that Kautsky so optimistically prophesied. What happened, as again and again in Russian thought, was merely that Western ideas and schools of thought were thoroughly revamped — often beyond recognition — to suit Russian circumstances.

The fate of Marxian revisionism in the Russia of the 1890's is a case in point. The legal Marxists as well as the theoretical economists alternated between denying and asserting their kinship with Bernstein's German revisionism. They were right in both instances. Western revisionism profoundly influenced and encouraged the Russian critics of orthodox Marxism. But the Russians' own ideas differed profoundly from those of the Germans. They had to; for what was suitable and plausible for German socialists, who remained honored members of a powerful party in an increasingly liberal society, would have been ludicrous in Russia.

The same parliamentary reform strategy that in Germany could be adopted by the Social Democratic Party itself, in Russia had to be assigned to liberals — or not at all. This was the predicament that the theoretical economists had to face, and they faced it in an unprecedented way by saying: by all means let the liberals do it, let them fight for gradual political reform. Likewise, a philosophical revision of Marxism in the direction of a neo-Kantian antirevolutionary idealism could be attempted inside the party in Germany, but not in Russia. And while the legal Marxists admired the progress-bringing powers of capitalism and of the "proletariat," they were far less comfortable with "paltry" conspiratorial Russian Marxists than with the flourishing and legal German Social Democrats. Hence a total rupture was as inevitable in Russia as it was avoidable in Germany. Caught between autocracy and an ultraorthodox revolutionary Marxism, Russia's "revisionists" disappointed both Kautsky and Bernstein.

If the ideological turmoil of the 1890's cannot be explained purely by influences from abroad, neither can it be understood as a direct triumph of Russian liberalism.

Liberal ideology had altered little from its mid-century faith in the Europeanization of Russia, and along with European liberalism it was readjusting itself only slowly to an industrial mass society. While Miliukov had asserted in the 1890's that "democratic liberalism of the newest type" was the heir to the westernizers of the 1840's, the lower intelligentsia of his own decade ruled otherwise. For socialism, not liberalism, continued to be the ideology of much of this intelligentsia, and the decade's ideological battleground. And while the rise of capitalism and urban labor had visibly shaken the populist belief in socialism built around the peasant commune, many of the intelligentsia's new westernizers, like Struve, turned first to Marx, not to Russia's liberals, as the prophet of progress via industrialization — and capitalism.

Nevertheless the nineties did result, if only indirectly, in a major liberal triumph growing out of the pro-liberal deviations within Russian socialism. True, these deviations did not increase the number of dues-paying liberals. But they made liberalism respectable, *hoffähig*, for the lower intelligentsia. For the first time, there existed an ideological rationale for collaborating with liberals — and for collaborating frequently and without embarrassment. Not a few in the intelligentsia remained socialist and were as ready to collaborate with revolutionary socialism as with liberalism. Yet now as never before, most of the lower intelligentsia had become a third force, unorganized but vast, between liberalism and revolutionary socialism. Events buffeted this intelligentsia between the two poles, but no longer was it moored to one and unalterably distant from the other. No longer did liberal meekness and the lower intelligentsia's intransigence alike make socialism appear the only pole.

Russian life was still too backward, too cheerless, and too

insecure to make liberal moderation and gradualism appealing to all of the intelligentsia. Yet the 1890's had transformed not only the life situation of the intelligentsia — now a booming professional middle class — but much of its ideology as well. As a third force, the lower intelligentsia was now at least a potential ally of Russian liberalism. To be sure, this was also the period when Russia's revolutionaries spawned an unprecedented organizational exclusiveness and ideological purism. But these were a tiny minority, whose sweeping later triumph has too often obscured an opposite trend within the Russian intelligentsia which was at the time considerably more important.*

* In the fifth volume of *A Study of History*, Arnold J. Toynbee concluded that "an intelligentsia is born to be unhappy. . . . Indeed, we might almost formulate a social 'law' to the effect that an intelligentsia's congenital unhappiness increases in acuteness in geometrical ratio with the arithmetical progress of time." The present reinterpretation of the Russian intelligentsia's evolution casts doubt on this Toynbee "law."

Chapter Four

FROM RIGHT TO LEFT

The first and main aim of the Union of Liberation is the political liberation of Russia. . . . In the realm of social-economic policy, the Union of Liberation will follow the same basic principle of democracy, making the direct goal of its activity the defense of the interests of the laboring masses.

First program of the Union of Liberation

Throughout the nineteenth century, Russian liberalism was not a movement. It was a state of mind, a hazy cluster of political ideals and programs, a few devoted activists plus a sizable outer rim of passive sympathizers. The picture changed quickly in the twentieth century. In its first few years, there emerged a large liberal movement, with its own organization, program, press. This movement did not enter upon the stage of history until the eve of the 1905 Revolution. The preceding years, the years 1901 to 1903, were a transition — a period of rapid but hardly observable growth, of internal, often clandestine crystallization, elaboration, expansion.

For Russian liberalism, these were eventful and unprecedented years. The liberals acquired powerful new weapons: first, in 1901, a magazine (*Osvobozhdenie*), then, two years later, an organization (the Union of Liberation). At last the shift was made from "small deeds" — mainly cultural and local — to the "senseless dreams" of national politics. And as the 1890's had foreshadowed, the gentry now began to yield its leadership of liberalism to the new intelligentsia, the professional middle class. Simultaneously, an unmistakable change occurred: Russian liberalism moved from right to left.

I

While the professional middle class, as already noted, is in some instances a slighted substitute for an underdeveloped business middle class, the differences between them throw as much light on Russian liberalism as the similarities. The business middle class espoused liberalism in the West — or in part of the West, part of the time — during the fluid, expansive, and relatively uncomplicated society of Europe's early industrialization. At that time, a passive, non-interventionist state was not merely a "bourgeois" utopia but quite plausible. Likewise, the political liberalism of the middle classes blossomed at a period when illiteracy, passivity, and timidity characterized the lower classes. The third estate, in claiming to speak for all of the population, in fact had in mind only the middle classes; the lower classes were not as yet capable of speaking for themselves or acting on their own.

Thus the liberalism of the West's business middle class combined the universal liberal symbols of individualism and liberty with specific class goals: in economics a passive, laissez-faire state, in politics an oligarchy rather than either an aristocracy or a democracy. Liberalism's universal symbols survived in Russia's new intelligentsia. But they were thoroughly altered by the differences between the early Western business middle class and the later Russian professional middle class.

If the West's "bourgeoisie" sought power when a laissez-faire state was still eminently feasible, the professions belonged to a later, far more complex stage of industrialism. Advanced industrialism forced the state, not only in Russia but (*mutatis mutandis*) in the West, to step in, to be the active instead of the passive partner of business. The rationalistic, efficiency-minded training and occupations of the professions alienated them all the more from the lingering laissez-faire ideals of business. Hence the professional middle class of advanced industrialism regarded an increasingly powerful state a reality that neither could nor should be opposed.

In the century or more between the ascendancy of the business middle class and the later flowering of a professional middle class, the West also saw the transformation of its lower classes. Slowly, painfully, incompletely, the lower classes of town and country entered the political arena. At first they did so only in moments of greatest unrest, of *jacquerie*-like eruptions at the height of liberal revolutions. But by the end of the nineteenth century, education, urbanization, technology — as well as new religious and secular movements — had readied the lower classes of the West for full and equal participation in political life. This meant democracy in its narrower political sense, and with it the broader democratic dreams of social and economic equality.

In the West, during the nineteenth century, the professions identified themselves as often with the democratic ideals of the underdog, of the lower classes, as with the oligarchic ideals of business and the landed nobility. Much depended on how well the ruling forces acceded to some of the modernist views of the professions and admitted them to a share of power and status. In Russia the lower intelligentsia and not a few in the upper saw little likelihood of this rise in position. The result was that this class remained more actively political than the professions in the West, and very soon — in fact, ahead of Russia's backward lower classes — made a total and permanent commitment to democracy, to the demand for political and also social and economic equity and equality. In an increasingly complex society, this in turn meant a welfare state rather than laissez faire.

Unlike Western business, Russia's professions thus readily embraced the notions of democracy and a non-laissez-faire state. And for the lower part of this class the liberal universals of individualism and liberty had to fuse not with laissez faire and oligarchy but with a later world view. In the nineteenth century such fusion seemed feasible only through socialism, or some brands of socialism. Not until the twentieth century could this be accomplished under the banner of liberalism, as a new generation of liberal leaders began injecting some of socialism's younger fervor and ideals into the declining appeal of classical liberalism. Only this new generation — Clemenceau and Lloyd George in the West, Petrunkevich and Miliukov in Russia — accepted wholeheartedly the new creeds of democracy, a welfare state, social and economic equity for the lower classes. This explains why in the nineteenth century Russia's lower intelligentsia was attracted more strongly, and earlier, to socialism than to liberalism.

The Western "bourgeoisie" was not the only class that found the new twentieth-century liberalism suspect and unappetizing. Russia's gentry, by virtue of tradition and class interest, was also wary. To be sure, a paternalistic autocracy and a placid business class had throughout Russian history vitiated laissez-faire schemes. But the gentry was less rationalistic and efficiency-minded than the professions. It remained rooted in the land and in a perennially local, traditionalist, and seemingly unchanging way of life. Like the peasantry, the gentry had little of the city's social fluidity, its quick tempo, its impersonal and formalized relationships. Even its liberal minority, therefore, craved local autonomy and tangible personal liberties above all else.

On the question of democracy, almost all of the gentry felt apprehensive. This apprehension stemmed in part from its own class interests, in part from a firsthand knowledge of the peasantry. Most of the gentry continued into the twentieth century to believe that the lower classes were unprepared for democracy, and that full and equal participation in the complex workings of a parliamentary system was a far-off ideal. The intelligentsia fervently asserted the opposite.

On which force should — and could — Russian liberalism rely? On the untried lower classes and the revolutionaries within the professions, who had already been tempting the lower classes with sweeping promises of democracy and social equality? On the gentry and the upper intelligentsia, with their traditional liberal emphasis on individual liberty and some political representation? Which would have a greater chance, a wave of militant mass demands or a more gentle urging by the country's educated and privileged minority? Should the change come only through the existing autocracy, through reforms from above? Or had a point been reached where only revolution, or a frank and convincing threat of revolution, could produce acceptable transformations? Together these dichotomies represented the old dilemma of liberal politics in an underdeveloped society.

II

In the opening years of the twentieth century, Russian liberalism was unwittingly aided again and again by an antiliberal government. In the late nineties the government entered upon an era of archconservative, contradictory, frequently inept policies not untypical of Nicholas II. These in turn stimulated sporadic local student, labor, and peasant unrests that did much to energize oppositional sentiment. At the same time, the government's increased wavering between its pro-industry policies of the 1890's and its pro-nobility policies of the 1900's helped the liberals by frightening or encouraging the gentry into militancy.

Inside the liberal movement, too, the ground had been somewhat prepared. Not only had the intelligentsia undergone an organizational and ideological transformation in the 1890's, but the liberal gentry also closed ranks. This happened only in the late nineties, after the zemstvo congresses convoked by Shipov had been repeatedly proscribed. In the lull that followed, a tiny group of the foremost liberals in the gentry formed a private group called the Symposium (*Beseda*). It was not to be a rallying point or a political party. It aimed, instead, at an exchange of views between leaders of different currents within the liberal gentry, focusing on zemstvo affairs.

Founded in Moscow in 1899, the Symposium functioned through leisurely, strictly private gatherings of two to four days. These were held in Moscow several times a year and were attended by ten to thirty of the Symposium's optimum membership of forty. Among the members were such leading slavophile liberals as Shipov; his Moscow associate, Khomiakov; and Mikhail Stakhovich, marshal of the nobility of the Orel province. Of the constitutionalists, the membership included Shakhovskoi and the Dolgorukov brothers, twin scions of an ancient aristocratic family who played an outstanding role in the years before 1905: the richer and more moderate Prince Pavel Dolgorukov (district marshal of the nobility near Moscow), and the militantly radical Prince Petr Dolgorukov (board chairman of the Kursk zemstvo). As an exception to its rule that members had to be landowners as well as zemstvo leaders, the

Symposium elected the lawyer and moderate constitutionalist Maklakov as its secretary.

The Symposium existed from 1899 until 1905. During its
first few years, the dearth of political life encouraged discussion and studies of routine zemstvo affairs. But when a
revival occurred, it was the Symposium that served as the
publicity-shy caucus for concrete zemstvo ventures: congresses, campaigns, new technical projects and groups. It
did so until the specifically constitutionalist organizations
took the initiative. Then the Symposium became less active
and contributed mainly through sponsorship of several large
liberal volumes on agrarian economics and politics.[1] Typically for the new atmosphere, the Symposium in the preparation and publication of these volumes worked closely with
leading intelligentsia liberals and reform socialists.

Also a product of joint gentry-intelligentsia efforts was the
liberals' first new organ in the twentieth century: the magazine *Osvobozhdenie* (Liberation). Already in the nineties,
Petrunkevich and his informal Moscow circle of constitutionalists had several times contemplated the publication of
a constitutionalist periodical in Western Europe. Now this
same Petrunkevich-led circle succeeded. After Miliukov
turned down the proffered editorship, it was accepted by
Struve. Recently banished to Tver, Struve was even then
thinking of emigrating abroad and publishing a magazine
there. To start publication, he received the large sum of
100,000 rubles, much of it from his earlier and also later
financial backer, the landowner Dmitri Zhukovski.

Throughout 1901, the actual appearance of *Osvobozhdenie* was preceded by much conferring, travelling, organizing of local contacts, and soliciting the blessing of leaders
in gentry and intelligentsia. Petrunkevich, Miliukov, Annenski all played active roles, as did Vasili Bogucharski, a

prominent writer and a historian of Russian revolutionary movements. Bogucharski's views evolved from populism to a revisionist Marxism, and now he followed his friend Struve into the liberal *Osvobozhdenie*.

The organizational preparations for *Osvobozhdenie* were aided by the new wave, also in 1901, of national and regional conferences of zemstvo, third element, and professional leaders. The first of these gatherings — the February 1901 Moscow Conference on Agricultural Assistance to the Local Economy — was indicative of the change from a lull to a period of renewed liberal activism.[2] But, although this conference was dominated by the traditionally militant third element and attracted some 360 participants, the organizing of *Osvobozhdenie* did not actually start until the next such conferences. These were the September 1901 Regional Conference on the Domestic Crafts, in Poltava, attended by over 200 zemstvo leaders; the tenth congress of Natural Scientists and Doctors, held in St. Petersburg during Christmas of 1901; and the March 1902 national exhibition in St. Petersburg of domestic crafts. At all these meetings *Osvobozhdenie*, its platform and its distribution, were busily discussed and promoted.

To the more private conclaves of key *Osvobozhdenie* sponsors, we have only one clue. This was the June 1901 *Osvobozhdenie* meeting in Moscow, which resulted in the circulation throughout the zemstvos of an appeal signed "Old Zemstvo Men" (*starye zemtsy*). This Moscow appeal centered on the forthcoming 1901 sessions of the province zemstvo assemblies. As before, bureaucracy rather than autocracy was attacked by name, and no mention was made of a constituent assembly or other nationally elected bodies. But the program urged for adoption by the zemstvo assemblies, as well as the general tone, differed drastically from earlier public statements by gentry constitutionalists. New, for one, is the Old Zemstvo Men's refusal to acknowledge the traditional idealization of the zemstvo. Instead, a skepticism and pessimism reminiscent of earlier socialist — not liberal — strictures imbued their 1901 appeal:

> The forty-year period that has passed since the beginning of the "great reforms" has led us to the same situation from which we departed forty years ago when beginning these reforms. . . . People are leaving the zemstvo, people who are deeply devoted to the zemstvo cause but have lost faith in the fruitfulness of work under present conditions. Replacing them is a zemstvo man of a new type, the opportunist. He cringes like a coward to preserve the name, the form of zemstvo institutions and finally destroys their value by ugly groveling before the administration. . . . In such a state of affairs, the relative insignificance of the material results of zemstvo activity is in no sense compensated by its educational significance. . . .

New, too, were the specific demands. A few months earlier, the February agrarian conference in Moscow had marked a turning point not only in activism but also in injecting a new theme into liberal zemstvo agitation; this theme reflected the democratic creed of third-element and gentry constitutionalists alike — and their gradual ascendancy in zemstvo affairs. The new demand was for a small zemstvo unit (*melkaia zemskaia edinitsa*). This meant extending the nonclass principle of zemstvo elections downward into the canton, where the peasants still existed apart, under different laws and different voting procedures. Endorsing this "small zemstvo unit" demand, the June appeal went still further in calling for the democratization of the zemstvo. This included

> the granting of identical electoral rights to all groups of the population without any class distinctions, with a considerable lowering of the electoral property census . . . the removal from the membership of the zemstvo of class representatives as such . . . complete equalization of the [peasants'] rights with the rights of other classes . . . equalizing the tax burden through progressive taxation of property income . . . on the condition that certain minimum incomes be exempt from taxation. . . .[3]

While the traditional liberal demands for personal and civil liberties recurred, the appeal of the Old Zemstvo Men on the also familiar topic of zemstvo autonomy was unprecedently aggressive and detailed: all government supervision should be removed, zemstvo jurisdiction should be extended to all local "benefits and needs," limitations of zemstvo taxation powers should be abolished. Sweeping independence was demanded for zemstvo activities in the fields of education, health, food supply activities, and statistical evaluations of property. Only elected zemstvo officials should hold office and represent zemstvos, and that without government approval. The same independence was demanded for hiring of zemstvo employees, the third element. The discussion of general national questions related to local affairs must be totally free, and zemstvo petitions without fail were to be considered by government agencies within a time limit. The various zemstvos were to have complete freedom to meet and work jointly.

Never before had such a complete catalogue of zemstvo woes been published together with remedies so specific and unconditional. The whole appeal exuded a spirit of democracy, militancy, and concreteness unknown in the small deeds era. Through this appeal, through the growing number of zemstvo and professional conferences, through the busy organizing of *Osvobozhdenie,* the year 1901 stood out as the beginning of the new liberal movement. Yet only the next year did these beginnings take form, inside Russia as well as in Struve's *Osvobozhdenie.*

The government itself provided a further stimulus early in 1902, when Witte's Ministry of Finance promulgated an ambitious undertaking, a nation-wide survey of agricultural problems. A Central Special Conference on the Needs of Agriculture established more than six hundred province and district committees to conduct hearings and report on local needs. These committees, whose scope was explicitly local, were headed by government officials, and their zemstvo representatives were appointed by the government.

In response, the liberals decided to convene an all-Russian congress of zemstvo officials. This decision issued from two earlier gatherings that were typical in being sponsored and organized by the government and devoted to narrowly technical problems: the March 1902 national exhibition on domestic crafts in St. Petersburg, and the Moscow conference on fire insurance early the next month. As in the Shipov meetings of the mid-nineties, participation was not to be based on political orientation and was to be independent of the government. But unlike the 1895 and 1896 congresses, this meeting was to include leaders other than chairmen of zemstvo boards. This big decision was further stimulated by new portents of unrest or reaction: the sensational assassination by revolutionaries of the Minister of the Interior, his replacement by a still more conservative official, and the peasant upheaval in the Poltava province.

The first all-Russian congress of zemstvo officials took place in Moscow in May 1902. The invitations had been extended by Shipov, then as in the nineties chairman of the Moscow zemstvo board, and the congress convened in his home. Fifty-two leaders from twenty-five provinces participated. This included fifteen chairmen of province zemstvo boards — slightly less than half, and the leading constitutionalist and slavophile liberals.[4] The mood of the first zemstvo congress was considerably less militant than that of the *Osvobozhdenie* gathering in Moscow a year earlier. The congress aimed at a compromise general statement for the guidance of individual zemstvo assemblies. More detailed additions, whether right or left, were voted down or merely noted.[5]

The two central issues were the conditions for zemstvo participation in the Special Conference on the Needs of Agriculture and the kind of platform to be pressed in its local committees. On participation, Petrunkevich first proposed a boycott by all zemstvo representatives not elected by their own assemblies, but this was modified to an appeal that zemstvo representatives be strictly elective. Despite differences on this issue, the prevailing moderate view reflected an unwillingness to declare open war on the government. The platform lacked the brusque finality of the Old Zemstvo Men's appeal, its ambivalence and haziness recalling rather the tortured semantics of the small deeds era. Yet the new emphasis of the Old Zemstvo Men recurred: a shift from specific to general demands, from gentry to peasant problems, from education to economic reforms. The first zemstvo congress echoed — albeit faintly — the 1901 *Osvobozhdenie* meeting, and its central theme went beyond small deeds:

The needs of agriculture can in no way be satisfied by separate individual measures. Above all it is essential to remove those over-all conditions that slow its general development. It is after their removal that individual measures in the area of agriculture may be outlined with hope for success.[6]

Most important was the convening of the congress itself, an unauthorized and united action by various currents of the liberal gentry. It established the pattern, the organizational form that up to 1905 would grow in importance, because it offered national co-ordination and a national arena for the zemstvo and its liberal gentry leaders.

For the constitutionalists, such a zemstvo congress furnished a much broader base than their own gatherings. But it also gave compromise a priority over militancy. That such collaboration with slavophiles and other moderate liberals would not be easy became apparent soon after the first zemstvo congress. When the tsar himself confidentially issued an official government reprimand to most participants in the congress,[7] the slavophile Stakhovich defended the congress as staunchly as the constitutionalist Geiden.[8] But Shipov allowed himself to be persuaded in lengthy interviews with the Minister of the Interior and the Minister of Finance[9] that the government harbored only the best intentions toward the zemstvo. As a result, he in turn convinced a rump Moscow gathering in July, a month after the congress, to remove from its recommendations the crucial demand for election, rather than appointment, of the zemstvo members of the Special Conference on the Needs of Agriculture. It was the platform thus modified that most zemstvo members presented to the local committees. Shipov himself soon became disenchanted with the government's promises, especially after its systematic harassment of outspoken zemstvo members on the Special Conference local committees. But the constitutionalists regarded Shipov's lapse into apostasy as an early lesson in the drawbacks of the zemstvo conferences, otherwise so ideal as a national coalition arena for the liberal gentry.

At about the same time as the first zemstvo congress, the first issue of the constitutionalists' own organ, *Osvobozhdenie*, appeared — on 18 June 1902 — in Stuttgart, where Struve had settled.* Three lengthy articles occupied the bulk of the issue. Struve led off with an editorial. The second major piece was a programmatic statement originally drafted by Miliukov ("From the Russian Constitutionalists"), and the last was "An Open Letter from a Group of Zemstvo Leaders." Written in the same vein, and evidently at the same time, were two related articles, which appeared soon afterward in *Osvobozhdenie:* "From Zemstvo Delegates," in the second issue, and Struve's "Liberalism and the So-called 'Revolutionary' Currents" in the seventh issue. Together, these five statements revealed even more about the initial views of the new liberal movement than did the Old Zemstvo Men appeal of a year earlier.

Struve's opening editorial statement dealt primarily not with the program of Russian liberalism, but with its relationship to the revolutionary movement:

> [*Osvobozhdenie* will address itself] not exclusively but in great measure to the moderate elements of Russian

* A semimonthly magazine, *Osvobozhdenie* consisted of sixteen large, closely printed pages. One edition, for clandestine distribution inside Russia, was printed on cigarette paper; a brick-colored cover distinguished the nonclandestine edition.

society not participating in the revolutionary struggle.
. . . But while the extreme currents in our country are
organized, the liberal-moderate nucleus of Russian society
remains in an almost amorphous state. . . . [The liberal
and revolutionary currents are parts of the same great
liberation movement, since] the struggle for freedom can
triumph only as a broad national movement, whose paths,
forms, and methods must be and cannot but be varied.
. . . The nonrevolutionary elements of society can only
have the right to appeal to the revolutionaries and to
divert them from violence and extremes [under one con-
dition]: when they have understood that *moderation ob-
ligates* [emphasis by Struve], when they themselves throw
political action and civic courage into the scale of history.

Struve clearly pleaded for unity with the revolutionaries.
He appealed to his liberal readers to recognize the great
contribution and potential of revolutionary currents, as well
as their own past weakness. In the seventh issue of *Osvobozhdenie,* on 18 September 1902, Struve detailed the same
theme. Addressing himself to the liberals, he stressed that

Sincere liberals must and will more and more understand that no matter how far they stood on many things
from the revolutionaries and socialists, revolutionary socialism cannot be to them what it is to a reactionary
government: "sedition." . . . Even twenty years ago it
should have been impossible to misunderstand the essence of the Russian revolutionary movement. It is above
all a healthy protest against political license by the government and its criminal neglect of the most immediate
needs of the popular masses.

Turning from liberals to revolutionaries, Struve preached the same message of reasonableness and unity:

> The day-to-day revolutionary struggle is accessible only to a very few, and the sphere of its immediate influence cannot but be limited. That is why such a vast importance attaches to moderate opposition and to all its legal organs, especially the press and zemstvo institutions. These organs in reality form the national consciousness and create lasting traditions. A disdainful attitude toward their great work is a major historical error and historical injustice.

Whereas Struve's task was to court revolutionaries and to minimize the mutual suspicions of radicals and liberals, the program drafted by Miliukov for the first issue followed a different objective. This program wooed the more conservative gentry. From the outset, the statement committed not only its signers but *Osvobozhdenie* as well to the zemstvo, to being close to it. For the zemstvo alone had means of action at its disposal, not only moral and intellectual but also political, since it was the organ of self-government in Russia. The program of the zemstvo must assure on the one hand parliamentary government, and on the other the support not only of the gentry but also of the professions in and out of the zemstvo.

After these definite commitments, the statement "From Russian Constitutionalists" postponed for further discussion in *Osvobozhdenie* two knotty issues: the nature of Russia's future constitution and its major social problems. But the statement did specify the manner in which parliamentary government was to be instituted. After the tsar proclaimed the personal and civil liberties demanded, the zemstvo's (and municipal dumas) rather than the government were to name representatives to an assembly to draft an electoral law. The third and final stage would be the popular election and organization of a national parliament. The statement closed with a specific rejection of the slavophile ideal of a consultative rather than legislative body: "free forms of political life are no more national than are the use of an alphabet or a printing press, of steam or electricity. They are simply the forms of advanced culture — sufficiently broad and flexible to contain within them heterogeneous national content."

It was characteristic of this initial phase of the new liberal movement that the Struve and Miliukov statements emphasized unity and broad principles. Except for a commitment to democracy, both sidestepped the more specific and thorny problems of tactics and social reforms. Uppermost was the hope that constitutional liberalism could unite around it the revolutionaries to the left and the nonconstitutionalist moderates to the right.

III

Within a year of *Osvobozhdenie's* debut in mid-1902, its original hopes for broad unity had to be modified. Struve's own numerous and lengthy comments wavered for months between urging greater militancy and smoothing over possible sources of discord. This continuing emphasis on unity was defended in the editor's survey of *Osvobozhdenie's* first half year. Rejecting the accusation of opportunism, Struve exclaimed that "we are forever gripped and tortured by thoughts of reconciling ideas with deeds, dreams and reality, idealism and realism, about the necessity of translating ideas into life and of breathing life into ideas." [10]

Very soon, this defense of *Osvobozhdenie* was sharply challenged by Miliukov. This occurred in a frequently quoted exchange in the seventeenth issue of the magazine, 16 February 1903, between *cc* (Miliukov) and Struve. Miliukov opened with the flat statement that

> Experience has shown that *Osvobozhdenie* is serving too large a circle of people and political currents to express precisely the opinions and attitudes of each. . . . The point is that, first of all, disagreements have already arisen and come to the surface. Furthermore, only confidence in each other can lead to that solidarity which is essential for co-ordinated action. The closer the moment of such action seems, the more important to discuss disagreements in time.

Miliukov objected in particular to the courting of the slavophile liberals. He protested against Struve's inclusion of Shipov, Khomiakov, and Stakhovich in an earlier discussion of the future liberal organization and against Struve's use of the slavophile term *zemskii sobor* (territorial congress) instead of parliament and constitution. Vagueness about program and tactics, he felt, was uncalled for — especially since the majority of the gentry might at any moment follow the slavophile liberals into a deal with a seemingly conciliatory government. Miliukov's recommendation: concentrate on organizing a homogeneous constitutionalist cadre and relinquish hopes of uniting the gentry around "an unclear slogan and unreliable, in part suspicious elements."

In this rare open confrontation of the two foremost theorists of twentieth-century Russian liberalism, Struve's rejoinder expressed no disagreement with Miliukov. On the contrary, it discussed precisely what slogans should be adapted by the "party" (this term was not used in the *cc* criticism) urged by Miliukov. Such a party must be con-

stitutionalist, thus excluding the slavophiles except possibly
as valuable allies, and it must be completely democratic. To
manifest this, and to insure complete support from all elements of the intelligentsia, Struve urged two changes in the
Osvobozhdenie position. One was in the realm of program:
the basic political demand should be broadened from an
assembly for drafting an electoral law to outright universal
suffrage, and social problems, agrarian and labor, should be
clarified. Struve's second specific plea concerned organization: the liberal party should aim at a skillful combination
of two methods of action, the legal and the illegal.

This rejoinder converted Miliukov's statement from criticism to stimulus, a stimulus for Struve's more specific elabo-
rations of Miliukov's own new position. As a result of both,
Osvobozhdenie's position crystallized and contracted. It
moved explicitly to the left, placing intelligentsia support
above that of the more moderate, slavophile-led majority in
the gentry. The Miliukov-Struve exchange on the nature of
the future liberal organization was followed within a few
months by the actual formation of this organization. In the
interim, however, the spring of 1903 witnessed further increases of activity in intelligentsia and gentry alike. A different action of the government provoked each.

In 1901 the populist-dominated Writers Union of St.
Petersburg had been outlawed, following its protest against
the March student suppression. Soon the left intelligentsia
had regrouped around a regular supper club headed by
what became known as the "culinary committee." The reform socialists of this culinary committee had been one of
the sponsoring groups of *Osvobozhdenie* and they continued
as active supporters. When, early in April 1903, much of
the world was shocked by the anti-Jewish pogroms in
Kishinev, the culinary committee convened a protest meet-

ing of more than 200 from the intelligentsia. Its resolution concentrated on the pogroms but concluded that "the Jewish question, like all the urgent problems of Russian life, can be solved only through free independent action of social forces." [11]

As the intelligentsia was being aroused and brought together by the Jewish pogrom, so the gentry reacted similarly to the government's February promise of major reforms, and the Minister of the Interior's antiliberal interpretation of the promise. The gentry responded by organizing a second zemstvo congress, the occasion being a government-convened St. Petersburg conference on a technical zemstvo problem — this time insurance. With Shipov again acting as initiator, the second zemstvo congress met in private St. Petersburg apartments in April, a few days after the intelligentsia rally. Half of the twenty-eight participants from seventeen provinces were board chairmen of province zemstvos. [12]

Both resolutions approved by this second zemstvo congress dealt with the government's February pronouncement and were to be sent to zemstvo assemblies for discussion and adoption. [13] The first resolution, approved unanimously, asked that prior to their promulgation all proposed reforms of local and zemstvo institutions be submitted for zemstvo approval. The second, approved after lengthy debate by the close vote of fifteen to thirteen, was suggested by Konstantin Arsenev, a leading St. Petersburg lawyer and gentry liberal, and for many years the most widely read contributor to *Vestnik Evropy*. Arsenev's resolution urged the government to include representatives elected by and from the zemstvos on each government commission dealing with the proposed new legislation. Despite Shipov's apprehensions, the marshals of the nobility — the ex-officio presidents of zemstvo assemblies — agreed to allow discussion of the resolutions, and they were approved by twenty-four of the thirty-four province assemblies.[14]

Neither of the April 1903 gatherings was directly connected with the founding two months later of the new liberal organization, the Union of Liberation. Their preoccupations and resolutions had been narrow and almost tame, very different from the *Osvobozhdenie* reorientation through Miliukov and Struve. But in trying to visualize the circumstances under which a nonrevolutionary oppositional organization came into existence under a traditional autocracy, we can hardly overestimate these 1903 meetings of intelligentsia and gentry, and the stir and emotions causing them. They, too, added to the liberal momentum, drive, and self-confidence, as did the 1901 beginnings and the first zemstvo congress and *Osvobozhdenie* issues in 1902. As in most of Russian life, the main stimulus in the founding of the new liberal organization was the government and its contradictory, wavering, usually illiberal policies since the turn of the century. Such policies did not encourage outright resistance. But they fostered increasingly the conviction, at least in the educated, politically-minded minority of the population, that something must change, something had to give. This vague but powerful new conviction explained the equally vague and no less powerful revival of oppositional activity: the political undertone of technical zemstvo and professional conferences, the leftward shift in liberal statements and leadership, the appearance and very rapid growth of *Osvobozhdenie*.

Like the general liberal revival, the new Union of Liberation remained below surface. It started as a clandestine group, with conspiratorial activities as well as unidentified leaders and branches; the autocracy was not shaky enough, and oppositional sentiment not strong enough, for anything more ambitious. Until the eve of the 1905 Revolution, the Union of Liberation therefore acted as constitutionalist headquarters, with a well-functioning cadre but no army. The Union of Liberation was conceived in July 1903 at a three-day meeting of constitutionalists leaders in Switzerland. Schaffhausen, a Swiss city near Lake Constance, was its home base, but for conspiratorial purposes each day was spent in a different mountain town nearby: Singen, Hohentwyl, Radolfzell. Twenty leaders attended the Schaffhausen meeting, according to Petrunkevich's memoirs, in which he emphasized the parity between "zemstvo" (meaning gentry) and "nonzemstvo" (intelligentsia) members:[15]

Zemstvo
1. Petrunkevich
2. Shakhovskoi
3. Petr Dolgorukov
4. Rodichev, a St. Petersburg lawyer since his banishment in the mid-nineties from the Tver zemstvo
5. Vladimir Vernadski, geology professor at the University of Moscow
6. Nikolai Lvov, wealthy landowner and moderate board chairman of Saratov zemstvo
7. Sergei Kotliarevski, law professor at the University of Moscow
8. Nikolai Kovalevski of Kharkov
9. Zhukovski (Struve's financial backer)
10. Petrunkevich's wife

Nonzemstvo
1. Struve

2. Pavel Novgorodtsev, law professor at the University of Moscow
3. Bulgakov, then an economics professor at the University of Kiev
4. Ivan Grevs, history professor at the University of St. Petersburg
5. Vasili Vodovozov, a Kiev journalist and political scientist
6. Bogdan Kistiakovski, a legal Marxist and journalist
7. Berdiaev
8. Semeon Frank, a legal Marxist and philosopher
9. Prokopovich
10. Kuskova

Petrunkevich's emphasis on the Schaffhausen parity between "zemstvo" and "nonzemstvo" was misleading, however. At the time, the term *zemtsy* (zemstvo men) usually referred to landowners. But, as the Petrunkevich list shows, at least three in the zemstvo half (Rodichev, Vernadski, Kotliarevski) were employed in the professions. Hence it is possible to make a more meaningful distinction, of three rather than two categories:

1. Gentry liberals (Petrunkevich and wife, Shakhovskoi, Dolgorukov, Lvov, Kovalevski, Zhukovski);
2. Intelligentsia liberals (Rodichev, Vernadski, Kotliarevski, Novgorodtsev, Grevs, Vodovozov);
3. Intelligentsia socialists (Struve, Bulgakov, Kistiakovski, Berdiaev, Frank, Prokopovich, Kuskova).

Such a regrouping reveals a balance more characteristic of the Union of Liberation. Dry and even irrelevant as such lists may seem, they bring out two other points as well. One is the absence of several prominent and later leading liberals from the professions, notably of course Miliukov (at the time lecturing in the United States) and the lawyers grouped around the actively liberal legal journal *Pravo*. The other is the Marxist coloration of the socialists. None of the subsequently so important populist leaders were present, not Annenski nor Peshekhonov nor Miakotin nor Gregori Shreider, soon to become one of the Union of Liberation's main organizers.

This uneven representation also underlines the preliminary nature of the Schaffhausen sessions. Conceived there, the organization was born half a year later, at the first formal congress of the Union of Liberation in St. Petersburg. But the decisions reached at Schaffhausen were later merely developed, not overturned. The first of these decisions was to organize not a party but a coalition of different currents, a federation of local groups. Even after the elimination of the gentry's slavophile liberals — symbolized by the Miliukov-Struve exchange in *Osvobozhdenie* — the proposed organization appeared too heterogeneous, especially to the gentry leaders present at Schaffhausen, to constitute a party. A second decision opened the Union of Liberation to any revolutionary socialists wishing to join. On this occasion, Petrunkevich first repeated Clemenceau's famous slogan, "no enemies on the left," and the majority sided with Struve against Rodichev in refusing to rebut revolutionary attacks.* Lastly, the Schaffhausen

---

* According to the lengthy unpublished history of the Union of Liberation by the participant Vodovozov. This work has a history of its own. Its author deposited it in the émigré Russian Historical Archive in Prague in the 1920's, before he committed suicide. In 1945, with the rest of this archive, Vodovozov's history was presented by the Czechoslovak government to the Soviet Academy of Sciences. While in Prague in the 1930's,

meeting broached a topic most important — and most touchy — for the nascent alliance between landowners and the urbanized professions:

For the first time a general discussion of the agrarian problem took place. It was recognized as essential to work out a definite plan for action on it. The appropriateness of government interference was accepted and the principle put forward (although within quite restricted limits) of forcible expropriation of land.[16]

Schaffhausen thus completed a second phase of the new liberal movement. The first phase, symbolized by the 1902 zemstvo congress and the early issues of *Osvobozhdenie*, emphasized on the one hand unity, and on the other the continuing predominance in liberal activities of gentry and zemstvo over the professions. In the second phase the *Osvobozhdenie* shift, the professional conferences, as well as the composition and decisions of the meeting at Schaffhausen, all demonstrate that unity had been replaced by the "no enemies on the left" theme, and that the intelligentsia's program and spokesmen were gaining over the gentry constitutionalists. But this trend, the trend from right to left, became concrete and unmistakable only after Schaffhausen, in the third and final phase of organizational crystallization.

IV

The half year between the Schaffhausen sessions and the first congress of the Union of Liberation was a period of intense organizing throughout Russia. The elaborate *Osvo-*

Professor Michael Karpovich of Harvard had made the only extant summary of Vodovozov's history. Two decades later, this summary was kindly transcribed for me by Karpovich.

bozhdenie network of contacts was further expanded, plans for local branches and liaison laid, tactics and programs discussed. By now the émigré *Osvobozhdenie* almost rivaled Herzen's legendary *Kolokol* of the mid-nineteenth century in influence, no less in the Russian nobility and inside the government than in the intelligentsia, and as chief liberal organ it displaced the "legal" *Vestnik Evropy* and *Russkie vedomosti.** Two regional zemstvo conferences also furthered the Union of Liberation's organizing drive. In August 1903 an agricultural conference in Iaroslavl was accompanied by an exhibition on popular education to which zemstvo representatives from all provinces were invited. Still more important was the all-Russian husbandry exhibition in September sponsored in Kharkov by its zemstvo and its Agricultural Society. A Union of Liberation meeting held there at the same time was attended by eighteen leaders from Southern Russia and the capitals, including its key organizers — Shakhovskoi, Kuskova, Bogucharski.

The Kharkov meeting devised a major organizational gambit of the Union of Liberation. Having relegated the gentry's slavophiles to the position of valuable but outside allies, the Union of Liberation still wanted to organize the more moderate constitutionalists among the gentry. Because the new organization itself was clandestine and hence illegal in Russia, many such moderates would not care to join it. Therefore the Kharkov meeting proposed what is currently called a front organization. The Union of Liberation was to sponsor a purely gentry and nonclandestine group that would not be officially linked to it. This group's

---

* In the fall of 1903 German police pressure forced Struve to move *Osvobozhdenie* from Stuttgart to Paris. At the time its circulation was estimated at eight thousand inside Russia and four thousand abroad. (Weber, "Zur Lage der bürgerlichen Demokratie," 237).

scope would be confined to promoting constitutionalist views and resolutions in the gentry-dominated zemstvo assemblies.

Less than two months after the Kharkov meetings, thirty or more leaders of the gentry gathered in Moscow for the first congress of this front organization, the Group of Zemstvo Constitutionalists. To distinguish its congresses from the general "Shipov" congresses, they were labeled "Novosiltsev" congresses, after their host in Moscow. This name itself was significant, for the host, Iu. A. Novosiltsev, was a district marshal of the nobility who never joined the Union of Liberation. Neither did other leading moderate constitutionalists like Count Geiden, the president of the St. Petersburg Economic Society, who now became active in the Group of Zemstvo Constitutionalists. Its limited and local mission was understood and even welcomed, as Geiden stressed later: "Our original task, which is far from exhausted, was to spread enlightenment locally, to try moving the provincial zemstvo assemblies to the left." [17]

This organizational separation of the Union of Liberation from the gentry's moderate constitutionalists, following as it did *Osvobozhdenie's* ideological ban on the slavophiles, decreased still further the role of the gentry in the new liberal movement. The first congress of the Union of Liberation clearly confirmed this trend. The intelligentsia's ascendancy was also given a boost by the coincidence of the first congress with two large specialized third-element conferences: the third congress on technical education, with 3000 participants, and the ninth congress of the Pirogov Society of Russian Doctors. These meetings brought together leaders of the intelligentsia from all over the country and affected the mood of the Union of Liberation congress by their presence and militant pronouncements. The role of the professions and the leftward trend within liberalism were likewise favored by the location of the congress not in Moscow, the traditional center of gentry and zemstvo, but in the more radical atmosphere of St. Petersburg, where the lower intelligentsia predominated.

The first congress of the Union of Liberation convened in St. Petersburg early in January of 1904 and lasted three days. The sessions took place in three private apartments, without any police incursions. About fifty participants — their names have never been published — came from twenty-two cities.[18] *

The congress started its deliberations by approving the name, Union of Liberation (*Soiuz osvobozhdeniia*). This title confirmed the earlier sentiment against a tighter-knit party, and it also acknowledged the organization's kinship to *Osvobozhdenie* (Liberation), although Struve's émigré journal remained independent. The congress then turned to the program of the Union of Liberation. Here some friction developed, and even the usually mild Shakhovskoi recalls "nagging questions and skeptical remarks," and having to pay passing tribute to "excessive doctrinairism." [19] It was finally agreed to postpone programmatic details until more experience had been gained. The populists then urged the Union of Liberation to confine itself to the gentry and the professions, leaving agitation among the lower classes to others. This proposal the congress rejected, as it did the hotly debated recommendation of the moderate gentry participants to eliminate a phrase about "defense of the interests of the laboring masses" lest it alienate less radical constitutionalists.

* In addition to St. Petersburg and Moscow, the cities were Chernigov, Iaroslavl, Iurev, Kharkov, Kiev, Kostroma, Kursk, Nizhnii Novgorod, Odessa, Orel, Samara, Saratov, Simferopol, Smolensk, Tambov, Tiflis, Tula, Vladimir, Vologda, Viatka.

The resulting program, the first adopted by the Union of Liberation, was brief and general, but outspoken:

The first and main aim of the Union of Liberation is the political liberation of Russia. Considering political liberty in even its most minimal form completely incompatible with the absolute character of the Russian monarchy, the Union will seek before all else the abolition of autocracy and the establishment in Russia of a constitutional regime. In determining the concrete forms in which a constitutional regime can be realized in Russia, the Union of Liberation will make all efforts to have the political problem resolved in the spirit of extensive democracy. Above all, it recognizes as fundamentally essential that the principles of universal, equal, secret, and direct elections be made the basis of the political reform.

Putting the political demands in the forefront, the Union of Liberation recognizes as essential the definition of its attitude in principle to the social-economic problems created by life itself. In the realm of social-economic policy, the Union of Liberation will follow the same basic principle of democracy, making the direct goal of its activity the defense of the interests of the laboring masses.

In the sphere of national questions, the Union recognizes the right of self-determination of different nationalities entering into the composition of the Russian state. In relation to Finland the Union supports the demand for the restoration of the [autonomous] status which existed in that country until its illegal abrogation.[20]

Despite its brevity, the Union of Liberation's first program left little doubt about the new orientation. The zemstvo received no mention, nor did the habitual pleas for local autonomy and personal liberties. Instead, the program flatly demanded "a constitutional regime." Paralleling this shift from the specific to the general, was the repeated, and novel, espousal of democracy. The program stated that all political reforms must be democratic and must include universal suffrage. Equally new and significant commitments followed in the realm of social and economic reforms. Novel, indeed, was the pledge that "the direct goal of its activity [is] the defense of the interests of the laboring masses." And the unqualified endorsement of the right of self-determination for all of Russia's nationalities had no precedent either.

After the adoption of the group's name and program, one item of business remained: its organizational structure. The only central body was to be a council, elected by secret ballot at the congress held at least once a year. The council could co-opt new members, and names of council members would not be announced. The local branches, organized either by area or profession, received broad autonomy. In addition to adopting these provisions, the congress heard lectures by three participants. One of them foreshadowed the organization's large-scale project of drafting a model constitution; the others dealt with foreign policy[21] and with the tactics of the liberal movement.[22]

The membership of the council of the Union of Liberation, elected by its first congress, conformed more closely to Petrunkevich's distinction between "zemstvo" and "non-zemstvo" than had the Schaffhausen meeting six months earlier:

Gentry
1. Petrunkevich

2. Petr Dolgorukov
3. Shakhovskoi
4. Nikolai Lvov
5. Kovalevski

Intelligentsia
1. Annenski
2. Bogucharski
3. Prokopovich
4. Peshekhonov
5. Bulgakov

Petrunkevich was elected chairman and Annenski vice-chairman;[23] Shakhovskoi became secretary and Pavel Dolgorukov fund-raising treasurer.

All the members from the gentry spent much of the year in Moscow, except Kovalevski of Kharkov, while, aside from Bulgakov of Kiev, those from the intelligentsia resided in St. Petersburg. This strict parity between gentry and intelligentsia appears the more striking since the gentry was in a distinct minority at the first congress, as at all subsequent ones. Of the gentry members, Lvov and Kovalevski stood out as considerably less radical than the others. Among the intelligentsia members, Annenski and Peshekhonov represented the *Russkoe bogatstvo* populists, Bulgakov was an erstwhile legal Marxist, Prokopovich an economist, and Bogucharski an ex-populist converted to both legal Marxism and economism.

The most striking thing about the council's composition is the absence of the liberal, nonsocialist intelligentsia. True, Miliukov was still abroad, but the council also failed to include even one of the half-dozen liberal professors at Schaffhausen. Subsequent elections and co-optation remedied this lack somewhat by adding I. V. Luchitski, a Kiev professor and moderate liberal mainly concerned with zemstvo and Ukrainian affairs; Aleksandr Maksimov, an editor of Moscow's eminent liberal *Russkie vedomosti*; and Iosif Gessen, editor of *Pravo* — the St. Petersburg law weekly which before 1905 became increasingly influential as *Osvobozhdenie's* domestic *succursale* (as Plehve correctly described it). Also added were Vasili Khizhniakov, a populist third-element leader who shifted from service as a zemstvo doctor to the key post of secretary of the St. Petersburg Economic Society, and L. I. Lutugin, a St. Petersburg professor of engineering, who, like Khizhniakov, was a very active reform socialist.

The national council of the Union of Liberation met about once a month, either in Moscow or St. Petersburg. Each of the capitals established a "technical commission" that carried out the organizational assignments of the council. Kuskova was the heart of the St. Petersburg "Big Group" and of its technical commission. With the reform socialists and lower intelligentsia in control in St. Petersburg, the emphasis there fell on the professions and on the task of circulating *Osvobozhdenie*. The leaders of the Big Group included Annenski, Prokopovich, Khizhniakov. Since all of them were officers of the Economic Society, and since its president, Geiden, maintained a benevolent neutrality, the facilities and personnel of the Economic Society became the Union of Liberation's base of operations in St. Petersburg. In the more staid and less socialist atmosphere of Moscow, the special "Group A" of gentry leaders and upper intelligentsia focused on zemstvo activities and on drafting a model constitution. As a technical base of operations, the Moscow counterpart to the Economic Society was the "professorial" daily *Russkie vedomosti*, with the heirs of the Morozov textile dynasty, Savva and Varvara, also aiding the Union of Liberation as they did the revolutionaries. As full-time secretary, Group A employed Grigori Shreider, an expert in municipal administration and a populist close to *Russkoe bogatstvo*. Shakhovskoi, as secretary of the Union of Liberation, maintained much of the Moscow–St. Petersburg contact through frequent trips, earning the nickname of the "flying Dutchman."

Obscurity seems to enshroud most organizations' technical day-to-day activities, and all too little was recorded about the actual functioning of the Union of Liberation. But it is known that in its role as a coalition rather than a homogeneous party — strictly confined by the caution and secrecy of all clandestine activity* — the Union of Liberation had little use for a large membership, mass following, or even for the provincial branches it had set up. Instead, most of what it did was accomplished by its few outstanding organizers, such as Shakhovskoi, Bogucharski, Kuskova, Shreider, Khizhniakov, and Lutugin. Whenever necessary they could draw, for *ad hoc* tasks, on a vast reserve of otherwise inactive sympathizers, the same kind of reserve that occasionally lent imposing effectiveness to tiny revolutionary sects.

Unlike the revolutionaries, the Union of Liberation had the benefit of yet another resource, the ideal transmission belt of zemstvo and professional organizations. It was now in the early 1900's, when Russian liberalism had finally created an efficient and vigorous organization of its own, that these arenas, once so unpolitical, became thoroughly politicized — by the Union of Liberation no less than by

---

* The only major brush with the authorities occurred in the fall of 1903, when Ariadna Tyrkova-Williams (then Borman) and a companion were arrested on the Finnish border with a large *Osvobozhdenie* shipment. The text of the court proceedings appeared in the *Pravo* of 4 July, 1904.

events themselves. At first circulating the illegal *Osvobozh-denie*; later drafting antigovernment statements and insuring their adoption by every conceivable zemstvo, gentry, and professional association; establishing, training, supplying local contacts; co-ordinating and caucusing, caucusing and co-ordinating: this was the kind of ubiquitous stage-managing and backstage wirepulling that best suited the times and the Union of Liberation's makeup and organization. In its few hectic years this type of activity was to characterize it throughout.

V

In its initial years from 1901 to 1903, the new liberal movement thus made its leftward turn unmistakably clear not only through its first program but also through its organizational structure. For most of the gentry's liberals, however, these years meant a continuation of the small deeds tradition. Again Shipov headed the zemstvo congress, and the emphasis remained on zemstvo autonomy and personal liberties. True enough, its own economic travails as well as stronger leftward currents made the gentry appear more concerned than before with the economic and social status of the peasantry. Hence the old self-absorption and the often patronizing philanthropy now on occasion gave way to such new gentry demands as the "small zemstvo unit" for equalizing the peasant's legal and political status. But only the hard core of constitutionalists around Petrunkevich was ready to follow the new liberal movement's left program. Organizationally, too, the clandestine, illegal nature of the Union of Liberation kept away most of the gentry and not a few upper intelligentsia liberals.

Yet if the program and organization had in the early years of the twentieth century resolved the right-left dilemma in terms of ends, the problem of means, of tactics, remained to torment the new liberal movement. Having itself decided to turn left, it was not nearly so certain about how best to eliminate autocracy, and with whose help. This persisting problem determined the very nature of the Union of Liberation's orientation. The program was blunt and novel, but it consistently avoided touchy problems such as the agrarian. And while the Union of Liberation's leaders and organizers were exclusively left, the Group of Zemstvo Constitutionalists and even the Shipov zemstvo congresses received much more public acclaim and attention from the Union of Liberation than its own clandestine activities and wooing of the left. Why?

A paradox appears here. The sweeping avowal of democracy by the liberal as well as socialist intelligentsia now impressed itself for the first time on Russian liberalism. Despite this, until the height of the 1905 Revolution the zemstvo — and hence the gentry — remained its central arena. To be sure, internally, in shaping the opposition's own climate of opinion, the various professional and third-element associations were more active and more influential. However, since no one in the new liberal movement had in mind mass revolution or a revolutionary *coup d'état*, the proposed reforms willy-nilly had to come from the existing government. And with this government the gentry and the zemstvo continued to carry infinitely more weight than had the recent (and for the government usually contumacious) intelligentsia associations. Aside from continuing government control and popular apathy, this was the main reason that the new liberal movement at times muffled and even camouflaged its own left orientation.

But within the liberal movement the left was also a problem. If the *apparatchiki*, the skilled technical managers of an organization, can be distinguished from its leaders and its spokesmen, the main apparatchiki of the Union of Liberation were almost all socialists. Shakhovskoi, the secretary of the Union of Liberation and still a militant ex-populist, stood out as the one exception. The socialists' leading role in the new liberal movement was not as illogical as it may appear. Inverting the Western pattern, Russian life made nineteenth-century socialism an earlier and more vigorous movement than liberalism. Thus revolutionary socialism inevitably offered a better school for clandestine apparatchiki than did small deeds liberalism. Equally important was socialism's great impact on all of European liberalism at the turn of the century, making it not only liberalism's great political rival but also a source of new ideas and zeal. To the Union of Liberation, too, its socialist apparatchiki brought not only conspiratorial skills but also ideas and zeal quite different from small deeds liberalism.

These socialist apparatchiki did not gain control of the new liberal movement and did not try to. Nor did they seek to exclude completely the liberal professions and gentry, ill at ease in the underground Union of Liberation itself. Such liberals played their main part in the multitudinous public, legal, "nonpolitical" arenas of Russian liberalism. Much read as *Osvobozhdenie* was, important and effective as the Union of Liberation gradually became as a small underground caucus, they were only one of the components of this rare combination of clandestine and public action. By itself the Union of Liberation during tranquil years would have been as isolated as the revolutionary sects had been, and the reform socialists understood this best of all. The problem was simply that the prominent presence of the socialists nourished in the Union of Liberation the seeds of its tactical uncertainty. While its moderate allies, the Group of Zemstvo Constitutionalists, aimed at influencing the gentry and conciliating the government, its socialist allies urged collaboration with revolutionaries and wooing the lower classes rather than the government. Likewise militating against any clear-cut tactical choices were the still slow pace of Russian politics, the youth of the liberal movement, its craving for unity, its temporary focus on underground organization and internal consolidation rather than on public or mass action.

These quiet but busy years witnessed basic changes within Russian liberalism, the changes from political ideals to a political movement, from the hegemony of the gentry to that of the intelligentsia, from "small deeds" to the "senseless dreams" of constitution and democracy. Now, not earlier or later, the lower intelligentsia's militancy replaced the gentry's prosaic gradualism. But tactically the transition years from 1901 to 1903 were barren. The new liberal movement was as deeply certain of its ends as it was hesitant and wavering about means. The old liberal dilemma thus remained unresolved. No more than the small deeds decades did the transition years of the early twentieth century find a third choice between conciliating autocracy and embracing revolution.

Chapter Five

PROLOGUE TO REVOLUTION

. . . to [Struve's question in 1894] of how I envisage getting out of the political impasse, I answered confidently: "Through an unauthorized meeting of zemstvo representatives which will demand a constitution."

Shakhovskoi

The Russian revolution of 1905 witnessed the simultaneous upheavals of five groups that in the West gained self-consciousness and then a share of power in separate and usually slower stages. In 1905, a "bourgeois revolution" coincided with a "proletarian revolution." The peasantry staged a *Jacquerie* of its own. Complicating all of these were not only an unexpectedly disastrous war but two novel nationalist upheavals — first a lesser one among Russia's national minorities and later a vast Great Russian counter-revolution by the monarchist petty bourgeoisie. Already in the prologue to this revolution, by the end of 1904, the combination of domestic crisis and stunning military debacles in the Russo-Japanese War created a new, sharply antigovernment mood in Russia. The rapid spread of this mood set off the 1905 Revolution.

True to the "anatomy" of most Western mass revolutions, the new mood was first echoed by the moderate — not the extreme — opposition. Hence the prologue to this, as to other revolutions, was stamped by liberal features and liberal demands. Accordingly, although the Bloody Sunday of January 9 is usually regarded as the beginning of the Russian revolution of 1905, the hazy divide was crossed not on that day, but two months earlier, in November 1904.

During that month a series of public manifestations crystallized public sentiment, brought into the open oppositional demands and organizations, dramatized the government's ever greater wavering and ineptness.

The month of November 1904 marked not only the prologue to revolution, but also the climax of the Union of Liberation's activity. For some time in 1905 this organization continued to play a role, but soon new groupings and the revolution itself superseded it. In November of 1904, however, it was the Union of Liberation which conceived and organized the two decisive public manifestations: a dramatic zemstvo congress and a nation-wide chain of intelligentsia banquets. Compared to the gore of Bloody Sunday and the burning countryside and strikebound cities of the following winter, a new zemstvo congress plus a series of intelligentsia banquets appear ludicrously tame. Yet in most revolutions small things precede the big ones, and the sensational finale usually follows many an undramatic act. In Russia decades had passed since the last large-scale stirring of public opposition. The liberal manifestations were the kind of prologue without which a revolution was inconceivable at the given time and place.

I

Within a month of the Union of Liberation's founding congress in January 1904, a national event shook the liberal movement and multiplied its potential. On February 8, the Japanese made a surprise attack on Russian warships at Port Arthur, and the Russo-Japanese War began. Defeat in war could lead to major national upheavals, and even without defeat the war made the government more dependent on public good will. In the short run, however, the outbreak of the war weakened rather than strengthened the liberal movement. For the unifying of any political groupings, especially heterogeneous ones, is never an easy task. And while cataclysms like a major war can at times aid such a coalescence, they can also inject powerful pressures toward division, as the extreme is radicalized and the moderates become more apprehensive and cautious.

Soon after the outbreak of the Russo-Japanese War, it became clear that such a polarization had occurred in the Union of Liberation. The potentially divisive issue was the war itself. The left in the Union of Liberation espoused one position toward it: as "defeatists" (*porazhentsy*), they were convinced that opponents of autocracy should hope for decisive military defeat by Russia; defeat would speed internal transformations, they felt, as nothing else might. Meantime, most liberals, plus a very few radicals, took the opposing view: as "defensists" (*oborontsy*), they continued to condemn autocracy and bureaucratic excess but felt that Russian victory was desirable. The positions of the defensists and defeatists seldom were openly voiced. Instead, they appealed indirectly through disputes over specific tactics.

The first clash occurred in *Osvobozhdenie* a month after the outbreak of the war, and involved once again the leading theorists of the liberal movement, Struve and Miliukov. The clash took the form of a letter to the editor by Miliukov, and a reply to it by Struve. Miliukov objected to Struve's first public reaction to the war, his much discussed "Letter to Students." Here Struve urged that the students, as representatives of the opposition, participate in patriotic demonstrations, adopt their slogans, "Long live the army" and "Long live Russia" — and then seek to add "Long live freedom" and "Long live a free Russia." Struve argued that

In the present difficult moment sharper and more belligerent slogans are out of place and hence undesirable. Now it is essential to stand firmly on that common ground created for all the Russian people by the national calamity — the war. For the sake of the great liberation task which demands the greatest possible unity, it is essential for you to treat with care and tact the uncomplicated patriotism of your friends, for whom Russian freedom is still an empty sound. Events and your persistent propaganda, I am convinced, will nurture a political sense among those capable of maturing.[1]

In strong words Miliukov objected to the opposition's hailing either the Russian government, which it strongly disliked, or even the army, as long as it served as a symbol and means of Russian expansionism. At the moment, he added, public demonstrations were narrowly limited to official patriotic slogans, while the opposition remained too weak to affect the political or military conduct of the war in the Far East. Its concern must be with the eventual, long-run relationship between government and public opinion. To keep itself free for this task, the present policy of the opposition should be "to stand aside."

Let us be patriots for ourselves and for the future, not worrying whether our patriotism will be recognized as such by [chauvinists]. . . . Let us not mix our shouts with theirs; no shouts at all — this is the most that can be asked of us no matter how difficult the circumstances.[2]

Miliukov's alternative slogan for the opposition was its old one: "Down with autocracy."

In his rejoinder, Struve stressed that the opposition did

not unanimously oppose the war. On the contrary, much of it shared the elemental patriotic sentiments of the rest of the population. Therefore the task of the opposition remained to merge the healthy strain in patriotism with appeals for reform. In addition, Struve justified his slogans, "Long live the army" and "Long live Russia," out of compassion for the soldiers being sent to death by the government, and above all because "we need a common ground with those who still do not understand us." Struve closed with a pointed remark to Miliukov. His own position, Struve emphasized, was not merely a tactical device but a fundamental goal — the long-standing goal of remaining in the main stream of political life even if it required "opportunism."

Inside Russia, the expression of the two positions voiced by Miliukov and Struve in *Osvobozhdenie* was more difficult because of censorship and patriotic feeling. Yet there did appear in *Pravo,* the St. Petersburg *"succursale"* of *Osvobozhdenie,* arguments for each of the positions. These statements emanated from leading figures in the Union of Liberation. Its chairman, Petrunkevich, provided an expression of the defensist position taken by Struve:

Of course, we cannot now suggest peace to Japan and must continue the war until Japan will agree to base the peace on conditions acceptable to us from the point of view both of our national dignity and of Russia's material interests. But without hesitation we must at the same time recognize [the following] in the name of humanity, in the name of the real interests of Russia: one must insist, for the sake of stopping the terrible bloodshed in the Far East, where hundreds of thousands of people are perishing, on abandoning all the interests of colonial policy. . . . Only in lawfulness and freedom can we find the conditions for might and genuine greatness of our motherland.[3]

A month later *Pravo* published a defeatist statement by Peshekhonov, a populist leader of the Union of Liberation. Going beyond Miliukov, he concluded with the same call for governmental transformation as Petrunkevich did. But in lieu of his patriotic theme, Peshekhonov wrote: "Examining my own patriotic feelings, I cannot say that they were offended by those defeats which Russian troops suffered in the Far East, and I am not a freak in this case. Around me I see many people who think and feel the same way." [4] Peshekhonov repeated with sympathy the slogan, "the worse, the better" (*chem khuzhe, tem luchshe*). This much quoted slogan mirrored the defeatists' conviction that the more military defeats Russia suffered the more likely fundamental domestic changes became.

The war also widened the division between intelligentsia and gentry organizationally. The St. Petersburg branch of the Union of Liberation, the stronghold of its intelligentsia, embraced defeatist views. The gentry's Group of Zemstvo Contitutionalists, championing the defensist position, declared at its second congress, in February 1904:

Due to the structure of our political life [the people] are not the managers of their own fate. The near-sighted policy of irresponsible authorities, cut off from the will of the people, resulted in a bloody denouement in the Far East. And now the support of the honor and glory of Russia lies upon the Russian people. They are called upon to sacrifice their belongings [and] sons to defend Russia from its enemies. To do this, to battle for Russia, is now a national task. "We are citizens of Russia" — that is the slogan of the day, that is what the national spirit must dictate. . . . *Only on the ground of popular representation,* in an organic unity of the monarch with the people, can Russia employ fully its long burgeoning forces and finally breathe freely.[5]

Thus, at the outset, the Russo-Japanese War had a negative impact on the liberal movement. The war shifted public interest away from domestic affairs; it made the future seem uncertain and unpredictable. Above all, it divided the Union of Liberation on an immediate and painful issue. The main result was that the enthusiastic organizing slowed down. Yet no open break occurred. The debate on the war continued — at times heatedly — in *Osvobozhdenie,* with the original Miliukov-Struve exchange followed by eleven more letters under the same heading of "War and the Russian Opposition."

But by the summer of 1904 a new position on the war issue emerged. The first indication of the new stand was another Miliukov article in *Osvobozhdenie,* coming half a year after the initial exchange between him and Struve.* This time Struve, in an editorial note, explicitly aligned himself with Miliukov's new position. Miliukov pleaded not against the war itself, but against letting the war obscure oppositional demands. The time had come, he said, for liberals to get busy on agreeing about these demands and on pressing them. According to Miliukov, liberals should demand a legislative national assembly elected directly by

---

* A third Miliukov-Struve encounter, probably the best known, came after the 1905 Revolution. Struve then appeared as a key contributor to *Vekhi,* a heatedly discussed collection of essays attacking the Russian intelligentsia for cosmopolitanism and irreligiosity. The next year, in 1910, Miliukov countered in another collection of essays, *Intelligentsiia v Rossii.*

the population rather than a consultative assembly chosen indirectly by the zemstvo and other existing institutions. Additional evidence that summer of a new position on the war took the form of a mass appeal circulated by the Union of Liberation throughout Russia, "The People and the War." The long appeal concluded:

> Enough of the people's blood, sweat, and tears has already been shed, without a murmur, on Russian soil. Now the people have also shed their blood silently in Chinese Manchuria and shed new tears for the fathers and brothers who went there. The people make the sacrifices of an unnecessary and ruinous war silently and obediently. [But] the people have the right to demand a removal of the present government of officials and make new arrangements. The people should destroy the single-handed autocratic rule of the tsar and his subordinate officials and win a constitution.

> Down with autocracy!
> Long live a constitution! [6]

The new position substituted the old erstwhile emphasis on reform for defensist and defeatist arguments alike. Hence the Miliukov article and the mass appeal neither praised the heroism of Russian soldiers, thereby endorsing the war, nor asserted that Russian defeats were of no concern and might further internal reforms.

Soon after this position on the war emerged in the summer of 1904, a new quickening began in Russian political life. Having been organized in the preceding quickening of 1901–1903, the Union of Liberation reached its climax in the second half of 1904, as part of a still greater revival.

This revival was touched off in July by the sensational assassination by Socialist Revolutionaries of the generally unpopular and archconservative Minister of the Interior, Plehve, and his replacement by the well-intentioned and considerably less conservative Prince Sviatopolk-Mirski. In October the revival was accelerated through a major defeat in the Russo-Japanese war, which led to the Japanese capture of the key Port Arthur.

The shock first of the assassination and then of the military debacle shook loose the general wartime passivity. And the greater receptivity of the new Minister of the Interior to reform and public discussion raised the hitherto drooping *élan* of the Union of Liberation. Thus for a second time a historical accident affected the evolution of the liberal movement. The first such accident was the founding of the Union of Liberation just before the Russo-Japanese War, rather than after its outbreak. The second, in mid-1904, was the shaping of a new position on the war issue on the very eve of a quickening of public life. Although the war had organizationally retarded and initially divided the Union of Liberation, the liberal movement was now not only reunited but equipped with a program, a nation-wide organizational network, and half a year of at least low-gear practical experience inside Russia. Much more than either of the revolutionary parties, new developments found the Union of Liberation ready to ride the rising tide of opposition.

II

The Union of Liberation's internal dispute on the war issue paralleled two other ventures during the political lull: a Paris conference of Russian oppositional groups and the drafting of a model constitution. Neither of these ventures influenced subsequent events decisively. But both confirmed the continuing tactical fluidity of the liberal movement, a fluidity which was to characterize the liberals throughout 1905.

The Paris conference of Russian opposition groups grew out of a proposal of the Polish Socialist Party at the 1904 Amsterdam Congress of the Socialist ("Second") International. Konni Zilliacus, of the recently founded Finnish Party of Active Resistance, extended the Polish proposal from socialist parties to all opposition groups, and eighteen liberal and socialist groups were invited. After initial acceptance, the Russian Social Democrats and most Marxist parties of Russia's national minorities refused to attend. Their refusal revolved around the unwillingness of the Social Democrats to participate as a minority, and charges linking the conference's Polish and Finnish initiators to official Japanese manipulations against its Russian foe.[7] Only eight of the eighteen groups actually sent representatives. Three of them were nonsocialist: the Finnish Party of Active Resistance, the Polish National League, and the Union of Liberation. Except for the Latvian Social Democratic Workers' Party, the rest were closer to revolutionary populism than to Marxism: the Russian Party of Socialist Revolutionaries, the Polish Socialist Party, the Georgian Party of Socialists-Federalists-Revolutionaries, the Armenian Revolutionary Federation. From a piquant source, and the most complete one on the conference — the Socialist Revolutionary Azev, unsurpassed as a double agent — we learn that the conference met for eight days early in September. Seventeen delegates participated, including Zilliacus; Roman Dmovski, the Polish leader; for the Socialist Revolutionaries — Chernov, the party leader, and Evno Azev; for the Union of Liberation — Struve, Miliukov,

Bogucharski, and Petr Dolgorukov, the less moderate of the twins.[8]

The nature of the Paris conference, and of the Russian liberals' participation in it, has been obfuscated by the fact that actually two meetings took place concurrently. According to the Socialist Revolutionary organ as well as Zilliacus' memoirs, the revolutionary parties met separately to establish a clandestine co-ordinating center inside Russia and to discuss joint revolutionary action.[9] This is confirmed by the Socialist Revolutionary announcement of the Paris conference, which opened with an appeal to workers signed only by the four participating populist parties.[10] On the other hand, the Union of Liberation, with the largest delegation at the conference and with Miliukov drafting both of its pronouncements, declared its continued preference for legal public manifestations. Hence the conference as a whole was able to agree only on a general declaration condemning autocracy and affirming the desirability for united action. Demands for socialism, a republic, and national independence were omitted, and the conference's declaration came closest to the Union of Liberation's minimum program of constitution and democracy:

> None of the parties represented at the meeting, in uniting for concerted action, thinks for a moment of abandoning any point of its particular program, or of the tactical methods of the struggle, which are adapted to the necessities, the forces, and the situation of the social elements, classes, or nationalities whose interests it represents. But, at the same time, all declare that the principles expressed below are recognized by all of them:
> 1. The abolition of autocracy; revocation of all the measures curtailing the constitutional rights of Finland.

2. The substitution for the autocracy of a democratic regime based on universal suffrage.

3. The right of every nationality to decide for itself; freedom of the national development, guaranteed by the law; suppression of all violence on the part of the Russian government as practiced against the different nationalities.

In the name of these fundamental principles, the parties represented at the conference will unite their efforts in order to hasten the inevitable fall of absolutism, which is equally incompatible with the realization of all the [fundamental] purposes pursued by each of the parties.[11]

The declaration's categorical emphasis on each group's total independence belies the later picture of the Paris conference as a formal alliance between revolutionaries and the liberal movement, as does the fact that no specific plans for future joint action were actually agreed upon. The Paris conference did accomplish something else. It reinforced the intelligentsia's most popular notion in the years before 1905, the notion of a united radical "liberation movement." The conference itself showed graphically that in fact no such liberation movement existed, beyond a minimum program and a mood. But in times of flux these can make all the difference. On the eve of 1905 most of the intelligentsia was more beholden to the idea of a liberation movement than to any specific organizations, liberal or revolutionary. Hence the Paris conference was a particularly happy compromise for the groups involved; it offered a symbol of collaboration while making no organizational or ideological commitments.

The second liberal venture in the 1904 lull was as prosaically concrete as the liberation movement (and the Paris conference) was symbolic. This was the drafting of a model constitution, which became known as the "Union of Liberation constitution." This document did not receive official endorsement by the organization. Vodovozov, the Kiev journalist who participated in the conference at Schaffhausen and became the secretary of the constitutional project, has emphasized that "the draft was not discussed at any general meeting of the Union of Liberation nor by any of its local groups, and was not adopted by the Union of Liberation as a whole." [12] But the Moscow and St. Petersburg branches of the Union of Liberation nominated the members of the constitution-drafting group, and in other ways too this first model constitution did originate within the Union of Liberation. Among its St. Petersburg authors were Annenski and two editors of *Pravo*, Vladimir Gessen and his younger cousin, Iosif Gessen. In the larger and more active Moscow group of participants, the leading figure was Fedor Kokoshkin — a young, brilliant, and fiery lawyer, ex-lecturer at the University of Moscow, and full-time member of the Moscow zemstvo board. The Moscow group also included two law professors at the University of Moscow, both Schaffhausen participants — Novgorodtsev and Kotliarevski — as well as Petrunkevich and the populist *apparatchik*, Shreider. Except for Annenski and Shreider, the authors of the draft constitution represented the liberal rather than the socialist element in the Union of Liberation.

Two different emphases characterized the draft constitution. One was the old liberal preference for continuity, institutional as well as procedural. Thus the Union of Liberation constitution spoke not of constitution but of the term already in use, "the fundamental state law of the Russian empire." More important, the draft constitution did not call for a republic or even a parliamentary monarchy. A limited monarchy of the German rather than the British type was deemed most plausible for Russia. Specifying the reigning dynasty, the draft constitution therefore gave the tsar sweeping powers. As summarized by the authors' own Explanatory Note:

> The Emperor has the right to impose a veto on legislation approved by both chambers, to appoint ministers, to declare war and peace, to hold the supreme command of naval and land forces of Russia, and to represent it before foreign powers. . . . Furthermore, the monarch through his first minister is given the right to dissolve the chambers.[13]

Stressed as much as continuity was the democratic program of the new liberal movement. The draft constitution repeatedly affirmed the favorite slogan of the "liberation movement": *chetyrekh-khvostka*, or "four-tail" suffrage — universal, direct, equal, and secret. Alongside the *chetyrekh-khvostka*, the draft constitution insisted on the other main democratic demand, a constituent assembly. Printed in large type for emphasis, the last paragraph stated:

> We consider that the only correct way for realizing the program outlined in this draft is to convoke a constituent assembly freely elected by universal, direct, equal and secret voting to work out and put into effect the Fundamental State Law. Only in this case will the law originate from the source commensurate with its importance — the will of the people.[14]

A mixture of juridical gradualism and unqualified political democracy, the draft constitution avoided the social and nationality problems and remained notably vague on the proposed functions and political powers of local self-government. Even more striking than the mixture itself was the continued tactical uncertainty that it reflected. Should the proposed constitution be granted readily by a reform-minded autocracy — or must it be extracted by mass pressure? Two other programmatic statements suggest that the draft constitution tried to provide for both approaches. These statements, published within a few months of the draft constitution, both originated from within the liberal movement — but with what a difference! For one of them moved as far to the right of the draft constitution as the other did to the left.

The press of other work accounted in part for the Union of Liberation's failure to discuss or approve the draft constitution formally. But equally decisive were the objections of its left element, which became evident in one of the two statements that followed the draft constitution. This was the lengthy official program of the Union of Liberation adopted by its third congress in March 1905.[15] The program repeated the draft constitution's "four-tail" suffrage and bill of rights demands, and was similarly vague about the details of governmental structure. Yet it went much further: it proposed extending the suffrage to women and called for separation of church and state. It was also considerably more detailed and sweeping on local self-government and the nationality problem. Above all, this new Union of Liberation program emphasized social reforms — mainly in education, fiscal policy, and peasant and labor problems — as the draft constitution had not done and probably could not have done.

If for the left within the Union of Liberation the draft constitution was too narrowly political and overemphasized institutional and procedural precedent, the second, later statement implied the opposite objection of the moderates: that the Union of Liberation constitution had departed too far, and too sweepingly, from the status quo. This second statement was the "Muromtsev constitution," a new draft prepared by Muromtsev, the eminent Moscow jurist and moderate liberal soon to become president of the first Duma. The July 1905 zemstvo congress "adopted in principle" Muromtsev's draft constitution. Thus it clearly represented better than the Union of Liberation constitution the outlook of the liberal gentry. Kokoshkin, Muromtsev's main associate in his constitutional project, had also been a key figure in the earlier draft constitution. He recalls that Muromtsev, "approving . . . the points of departure of the 'Union of Liberation constitution,' was not completely satisfied with the editing of the project, with the grouping of the material, with the location of sections. . . ." [16]

Yet style was not the main point at issue. Muromtsev's model constitution aimed not at replacing the existing laws but at being substituted smoothly and easily by the present authorities for specific sections of the statutes in force. Muromtsev minimized changes from the existing legislation, and phrased such changes in still more legalistic and formal language than that of the earlier draft constitution. To be sure, the spirit remained the same, and the sections on the legislature appeared even more thorough and workable. But in line with his whole emphasis on a new statute that the existing government could promulgate without inviting a drastic transformation, Muromtsev omitted mention of the constituent assembly — that Pandora's box which no conservative state would willingly place in the hands of a turbulent populace. [17]

Even as modified by the divergent Muromtsev constitution and the Union of Liberation program, the "Union of Liberation constitution," as well as the Paris conference, continued the crystallization of the liberal movement's position. Both reaffirmed constitution and democracy as the Union of Liberation's main battle cry. If these two ventures remained inconsequential, it was not only because they took place during a political lull, but also because the Union of Liberation was itself still wavering between left and right.

A change came early in the fall, when the Union of Liberation for the first time decided upon large-scale public manifestations. With the new Minister of the Interior, Sviatopork-Mirski, promising a government based on "public confidence" and proclaiming a "springtime" of enlightenment, the St. Petersburg *Pravo* replaced the far-off *Osvobozhdenie* as the main organ of the Union of Liberation. *Pravo's* thinly disguised constitutional slogan — "reform, not reforms" — was much repeated. Soon the Union of Liberation also acquired two daily newspapers in St. Petersburg, the first of many to spring up during the revolution. The staff of *Nasha zhizn* represented the revisionist Marxist leaders of the St. Petersburg Union of Liberation. In *Syn otechestva*, the *Russkoe bogatstvo* populists at first collaborated with the intelligentsia's liberals, such as the *Pravo* managing editor, M. I. Ganfman, and only later with the Socialist Revolutionary leadership. Beginning publication on the eve of the November manifestations, *Nasha zhizn* and *Syn otechestva*, albeit to the left of *Pravo*, likewise concentrated at the outset on constitutional demands and on the Union of Liberation's plans.

These ambitious plans dominated the Union of Liberation's second congress, convened late in October 1904. Like the first congress, it met in St. Petersburg with the same number of participants and the same geographical distribution.* But events of the intervening eight months had encouraged a drastic reversal from clandestine preparatory work to large-scale public activity. The second congress thus resolved

1. To take a most active part in the forthcoming congress of zemstvo and municipal leaders and to make all efforts to move it in the direction of open declarations of constitutional demands.

2. In consideration of the fortieth anniversary of the court [reforms] on November 20, to organize banquets on that day through its members in St. Petersburg, Moscow, and in as many cities as possible. Constitutional and democratic resolutions must be adopted, composed in a much more decisive tone than those that can be expected from the congress of zemstvo and municipal leaders.

3. To raise through its zemstvo members in the forthcoming district and province assemblies the question of

---

* The Union of Liberation's two later congresses met in Moscow but were similar in number of participants (about fifty), cities represented (some two dozen) — and in immunity from police interference. The third congress, in March 1905, focused on the extensive new Union of Liberation program. (According to Miliukov ["Rokovye gody," January 1939, 125], half a year later this program was adopted with only slight revisions by the Constitutional Democratic party.) In August 1905 the fourth and last congress was highlighted by two decisions: tactically the reluctant participation in the proposed consultative "Bulygin duma"; organizationally the establishment of the Constitutional Democratic Party. The earlier congresses were unreported at the time, but the *Osvobozhdenie* of September 26 reproduced the resolutions of the fourth congress while the next issue carried an extensive report by "the Secretary of the Congress." Never formally dissolved, the Union of Liberation largely stopped functioning by mid-October 1905, when the government's October Manifesto and political amnesty were published and the Constitutional Democratic Party held its first congress. Even three months earlier, in the *Osvobozhdenie* of 13 July, Miliukov complained that the newer, revolution-spawned political groupings were judging the Union of Liberation by the more moderate of its allies instead of its own pre-1905 militancy.

introducing in Russia a constitutional system and of the necessity of convening for this purpose a popular assembly on a broadly democratic basis.[18]

III

In the prologue of the revolution, the second zemstvo congress of November 1904 had a decisive impact on the country as a whole. For the history of Russian liberalism, this zemstvo congress also provides an exceptionally detailed and complete picture of the different types of gentry liberals and their outlook at the start of the 1905 Revolution. Fascinating, too, are the glimpses it offers into government tactics, formal and informal.

The first zemstvo congress, of May 1902, had set up an organizational bureau for future zemstvo congresses, located in the Moscow zemstvo and headed by Shipov. This bureau had done nothing until two gentry members of the Union of Liberation's national council approached it in August of 1904 about convoking another zemstvo congress. The response was a quick affirmative, and not merely because of the new Minister of the Interior's "springtime," but also because of the new complexion of the bureau. Prior to his assassination the preceding Minister of the Interior had barred Shipov from re-election as board chairman of the Moscow zemstvo, and in the spring of 1904 the provincial assembly had replaced him with the constitutionalist F. A. Golovin, a moderate who in 1907 succeeded Muromtsev as president of the Duma. Golovin, less conciliatory toward the government than Shipov, gave the congress bureau a constitutionalist coloration. Shipov, who remained chairman of the bureau, testified that "all [bureau members] except me were convinced constitutionalists and in large part belonged to the Union of Liberation." [19]

Early in September, Golovin convened the first meeting of the congress bureau, which unanimously agreed to issue a call for a zemstvo congress early in November 1904. Its first agenda was limited to zemstvo affairs, but the following week — after the Minister of Interior's famous "public confidence" speech — the bureau broadened the agenda somewhat. When its constitutionalist members also insisted on a discussion of broad political reforms, Shipov threatened to resign his chairmanship if the bureau worded its draft resolution on the subject too specifically. The bureau accepted his condition and assigned the resolution to an editorial committee headed by the Kursk zemstvo delegate, Viacheslav Iakushkin, a professional historian and member of the Union of Liberation. The other members were Shipov and Kokoshkin, the Union of Liberation legal specialist who played a key role in preparing both the Union of Liberation and the Muromtsev model constitutions.

With a split thus narrowly averted inside the congress bureau, an unexpected development took place the next month — one that touched off a revealing series of maneuvers between zemstvo leaders and the government. Informed by his assistant on zemstvo affairs that a congress was planned, the new Minister of the Interior procured a speedy approval from the tsar on condition that the congress be held in St. Petersburg, not Moscow. But what the minister proposed and the tsar approved differed considerably from the plans already made by the bureau; the government had in mind a congress like those of the nineties, including only board chairmen and dealing exclusively with technical zemstvo affairs. In the meantime, however, the tsar's approval of the congress became generally known and made a vast impression. Invitations to the congress implied government approval, which undoubtedly increased the prestige and attendance of the congress.

Complications emerged during Shipov's first interview with the Minister of the Interior at the end of October. When Shipov showed him first the list of invited zemstvo leaders and then the draft resolution, the minister replied that he himself would sign the resolution immediately with both hands. But, Sviatopolk-Mirski added, the resolution's adoption by the zemstvo congress would be tantamount to his dismissal from his key post. Shipov argued insistently in favor of the bureau's plan for the congress, and the minister finally agreed that it was too late to call it off and that he would urge the tsar to approve. A few days thereafter, the congress bureau at an extensive meeting decided to hold the congress whether or not the government granted permission. It also adopted a third and still broader agenda, and added a new, more radical conclusion to the draft resolution.

The last meeting of the congress bureau was attended by Petrunkevich, who had previously been banned from St. Petersburg since his 1879 arrest. His presence provided the gentry's constitutionalists with the only leadership held to be equal to Shipov's, and his habitual combativeness did much to push the preparations and the congress itself leftward. Yet so great was Shipov's prestige that at this meeting of the congress bureau its constitutionalist majority once again retreated in the face of another threat that he would otherwise resign. Again the bureau modified the wording of the draft resolution. On its controversial paragraph dealing with the future political structure of Russia, the bureau now agreed to submit two versions: the majority's constitutionalist version and a more moderate one that did not conflict with Shipov's slavophile views.

On the last day of October the Minister of the Interior received as the bureau's delegation Shipov, Petrunkevich, and Prince Georgi Lvov.* Sviatopolk-Mirski urged them to postpone the meeting, at least to hold it in a provincial city, or as a last resort to withdraw the draft resolution's paragraph calling for freedom of speech, press, and other civil rights. The delegation rejected all three of these demands. The next day the minister informed the delegation that the tsar refused to approve the congress, since it deviated both in scope and in composition from a conference of zemstvo board chairmen. When asked by the three delegates whether a private gathering of zemstvo leaders would be acceptable, the minister replied that no law prohibited private gatherings and that the police would not prevent a privately convened zemstvo congress.

On the very eve of the zemstvo congress itself — in November 1904 — the Group of Zemstvo Constitutionalists met in Moscow for its third congress. An advance meeting in St. Petersburg had been deeply impressed by Miliukov, then stopping in Russia between the Paris conference and long-scheduled lectures at the University of Chicago. Miliukov gave an eyewitness account of the new constitutional regime in Bulgaria, and this precedent of backward Bulgaria moved Geiden and other moderates to support immediate demands for a constitution. Thus the third congress of the Group of Zemstvo Constitutionalists assured a firmly constitutionalist majority at the zemstvo congress the following month.

After three months of negotiating and caucusing, this zemstvo congress met as scheduled, in different private

---

* Prince Lvov was a moderate constitutionalist who then served as board chairman of the Tula zemstvo and in 1917 became first head of the Provisional Government. He is not to be confused with Nikolai Lvov, another zemstvo leader and moderate constitutionalist, who was one of the founders of the Union of Liberation at Schaffhausen.

houses in St. Petersburg, from November 6 through November 9. The number present underscored the prominence of this congress as compared to its predecessors. The first zemstvo congress, in May 1902, had been attended by fifty-two leaders from twenty-five provinces, including fifteen chairmen of province zemstvo boards; and the smaller second zemstvo congress, in April 1903, by twenty-eight, including fourteen board chairmen, from seventeen provinces. The third zemstvo congress doubled and trebled these figures. More than one hundred invited delegates came from thirty-three of the thirty-four provinces that had zemstvo institutions, and among them were thirty board chairmen, the elected full-time executives of the province zemstvos.[20] This congress brought together the leading figures of gentry liberalism: the slavophiles Shipov, Khomiakov, Stakhovich; the Union of Liberation leaders Petrunkevich, Shakhovskoi, Rodichev, Petr Dolgorukov, Zhukovski, Nikolai Lvov, Kokoshkin; the moderate constitutionalists Muromtsev, Georgi Lvov, Novosiltsev, Geiden. Shipov was elected congress chairman, while the other congress officers were Petrunkevich, Kokoshkin, and three moderate constitutionalists.

The congress regarded its meeting as an event of epochal significance. At a critical moment in Russian history, this gathering — unrepresentative as it was — had to speak for all of Russia. Now the whole congress believed Shakhovskoi's decade-old prophecy that zemstvo leaders could and should break the political impasse by meeting on their own and voicing bold constitutional demands. Hence the draft resolution prepared by the congress bureau became the main item of business and occupied three entire days.[21] No other discussion and no other document provided so clear a picture of the liberal gentry's political mood and attitudes.

During the initial session of the congress, on November 6,

the first four points of this draft resolution were adopted quickly and unanimously:

1. The abnormality of the state's existing administrative system has manifested itself especially since the beginning of the 1880's. This abnormality consists in the complete separation of the government from the public and the absence of that mutual confidence that is essential for national life.

2. The relationship of the government to the public has been based on the fear of developing political independence and the constant effort to prevent the people from participating in the administration of the state. Proceeding from these premises, the government has sought to institute administrative centralization in all branches of local government, and to control all aspects of public life. Relations with the public have been maintained by the government exclusively in terms of bringing the activities of public institutions in line with the views of the government.

3. The bureaucratic system, separating the supreme authority from the population, creates the basis for numerous occasions of arbitrary and personal abuse. Under such a system, the public lacks the ever essential assurance of strict protection of each individual's lawful rights, and its confidence in the government is undermined.

4. The regular flow and development of state and public life is possible only under the condition of an active and close contact, of unification of the state authority with society.

The fifth point of the resolution, dealing with individual rights, provoked a lengthy discussion by the various legal experts present; mostly theoretical, the discussion centered on the question of how to insure the government's adherence to the demanded laws. As a result, the revised version added a demand for legal provisions by which officials violating such rights would be prosecuted and punished:

5. To prevent possible occurrences of administrative license, it is essential to establish and carry out consistently the principles of the inviolability of the individual and of private domicile. Without a ruling by an independent court authority no one should be subjected to search or limited in his rights. For the purpose indicated above it is essential, furthermore, that procedures be established for civil and criminal prosecution of officials violating the law to insure the practical realization of the principles of lawfulness in administration.

In point 6 only minor and stylistic changes were made, the final version reading as follows:

6. For the full development of the spiritual forces of the people, for a universal clarification of popular needs, and for the unobstructed expression of public opinion, it is essential to provide freedom of conscience and religion, freedom of speech and press, and also freedom of assembly and association.

Point 7 of the draft resolution dealt with the peasant problem, and it, too, entailed lengthy discussions. Aside from diffuse and technical arguments, most participants agreed that the peasantry as the overwhelming majority of the population represented a problem that deserved to be noted separately. The bureau's original version was therefore adopted as point 8 with a new point 7 added:

7. The individual, civil, and political rights of all citizens of the Russian empire must be equal.

8. The independence of the public is the main condition for a proper and successful development of the country's political and economic life. Since a considerable majority of Russia's population belongs to the peasant estate, it is therefore necessary to begin by putting the latter in a position in which it can develop initiative and energy. This can be achieved only through a fundamental change of the present wrong and degraded condition of peasants. For this purpose it is essential:

(a) to make the peasants equal in individual rights with persons of other estates;

(b) to free the village population from administrative tutelage in all aspects of its personal and public life;

(c) to protect it through a proper system of courts.

On the next point of the draft resolution, concerning local self-government, lengthy debate again ensued. As on previous occasions, much of it dealt with style or the question of how detailed the resolution could and should be. Three provisions were added to the draft version. Of these, one was the inclusion of municipal self-government (the dumas), another extended the resolution to all parts of Russia, and the last specified the demand that self-government be given jurisdiction over all local questions. In its final form the point reads as follows:

9. Zemstvo and municipal institutions, in which local public life is mainly concentrated, must be put in a position where they can successfully fulfill the responsibilities appropriate for properly and broadly organized organs of self-government. For this the following is essential:

(a) that zemstvo representation be based not on class lines [but rather] that to the extent possible all available elements of the local population be drawn into participation in zemstvo and municipal self-government;

(b) that zemstvo institutions be brought [closer] to the population through the creation of small zemstvo units along lines guaranteeing their actual independence;

(c) that the sphere of jurisdiction of zemstvo and municipal institutions be extended to all areas of local welfare and needs;

(d) that the aforesaid institutions be granted the required stability and independence. Only if these exist is the correct development of their activities possible and the creation of the proper relations between governmental and public institutions.

[e] [that] local self-government should be extended to all parts of Russia.

The congress adopted the first nine points of the resolution by the middle of its second day. Then came the apogee, as the congress turned to the more general points 10 and 11, which dealt with the future political structure of Russia. On these points the liberal gentry had always been most deeply divided between its constitutionalists and slavophiles, and it was on this question that the preparations for the third zemstvo congress had nearly floundered. The fact that Shipov, although a member of a distinct minority, was universally revered in zemstvo circles, lent additional drama to the impending debate.

Petrunkevich, the first to speak in this central debate, noted that he himself belonged to a minority within the congress bureau. This minority had favored a specific demand for constitutional government. But the majority had approved a formula acceptable to all elements — meaning slavophiles as well as constitutionalists. In the ensuing debate the battle lines were thus drawn between the draft resolution and the explicitly constitutionalist version first urged in Petrunkevich's long speech. He was seconded by Rodichev and most strongly by Lev Briukhatov, a Tambov board member and congress officer:

> [The only possible] solution is the limitation of autocracy and its replacement by a constitutional system. This must be clearly expressed in the resolution. There is no reason to fear dreadful words. . . . There is no reason at this time to take the slavophile current into consideration.[22]

Shipov, the only slavophile to speak, made a long and deeply felt rejoinder. He reiterated his faith in ethical social principles rather than law, and his belief that the Russian people were different from those of the West. His speech was a strong defense of the slavophile position in general.[23] After several constitutionalists had spoken, two Union of Liberation leaders — Petr Dolgorukov and Nikolai Lvov — renewed the bureau's proposal that the resolution include both a majority and minority statement on this central issue, and the proposal was accepted.

Point 10 required four separate ballots. The first showed that 71 favored the majority resolution and 27 the minority. The next three ballots dealt with specific additions to the majority resolution, which represented not Petrunkevich's version but the original draft without the word "constitution." Everyone present voted on the additions, including the minority in the first ballot. The second vote, on popular representatives participating in legislation, was carried by

60 to 38. The next question — the participation of popular representatives in controlling the government's income and expenditures — was approved by 91 to 7. Last came the approval of participation by popular representatives in supervising the legality of actions by the administration, 95 to 3. Point 10 appears as follows in published form:

10. But in order to create and preserve an always active and close contact and unity of the state with society, on the basis of the above principles guaranteeing the proper development of state and public life, the following is absolutely essential:

Opinion of the Majority	*Opinion of the Minority*
the regular participation of popular representatives, in a distinct elected institution, in carrying out legislative functions, in establishing a state budget of income and expenditures, and in supervising the legality of the administration's actions.	the regular participation in legislation of popular representatives in a distinct elected institution.

At the outset of the third day, point 10 as quoted above was formally approved with only seven negative votes. Thereupon followed the hardly less controversial final point of the resolution. This dealt with the means of putting the reforms into effect. Two leaders of the Union of Liberation, first Nikolai Lvov and then Kokoshkin, spoke out strongly against the draft resolution's implied demand for a constituent assembly. Both felt that the need for a constitutent assembly grows out of a state of anarchy only, when no state authority is effective. At the moment, they said, such a state authority did exist, and its opponents were not powerful. Therefore the facts must be faced and the achievement of the proposed reforms sought through the tsar. In a rejoinder, Petrunkevich disclaimed any demand for a constituent assembly, so long as "the people" were allowed to share with the government in the lawmaking.[24] The long debate ended by the adoption, with only two opposing votes, of a version offered by Petrunkevich as coming from the chairman and three vice-chairmen of the congress:

11. In view of the importance and difficulty of external and internal conditions being experienced by Russia, the private conference expressed the [following] hope: that the supreme authority call together freely elected representatives of the people, in order to lead our fatherland with their collaboration on a new path of state development, of establishing principles of law and interaction between state and people.[25]

While the congress was in session, the police had not interfered with it nor entered its premises. The one governmental obstruction occurred on the very eve of the congress, when the press was ordered to make no further mention of it. Moreover, the Minister of the Interior rejected a formal presentation of its resolution, but stated that he would accept the resolution if presented by Shipov alone. After the delegation had approved this procedure, Shipov complied in a second interview. During this lengthy meeting, Sviatopolk-Mirski voiced complete agreement with the main eleven-point resolution of the third zemstvo congress. On the majority and minority resolutions of Point 10, he said several times that he could not see a substantive difference, but that he sympathized with the minority. He promised to present the resolution to the tsar and asked Shipov to have a general memorandum prepared. This task was undertaken by a dozen leading zemstvo figures in Moscow, including Shipov, leaders of the Union of Liberation, and also moderate constitutionalists. The memorandum was actually written by Prince Sergei Trubetskoi, an influential moderate constitutionalist, a religious mystic and a philosophy professor at the University of Moscow. During the 1905 Revolution Trubetskoi skyrocketed to national eminence in the few months between June, when he delivered a famous speech to the tsar in the name of the May zemstvo congress,[26] and September, when his election as first president (rector) of the newly self-governing University of Moscow was followed within a few weeks by his death at the age of forty-three.

The Trubetskoi memorandum, reflecting the views of key liberals in the gentry, did much to clarify the outlook of the third zemstvo congress. Written as an impassioned appeal to Nicholas II personally, the memorandum concentrated on two points. One of these stressed that fundamental reforms had been made unavoidable by the Russo-Japanese War, and that these reforms were unthinkable without replacement of bureaucratic absolutism by political freedom. The memorandum specifically mentioned peasant reforms and their urgency, but once again it designated political freedom as the essential first step:

> But either all of these reforms presuppose political freedom, a legal system of state life, and correctly organized popular representation — or the reforms cannot be properly worked out, realized and translated into

life. . . . The center of gravity in the question of arranging the economic and civil life of the peasants has been shifted to the general question of the old and new regime . . . the rights and lack of rights not of the village but of all Russian citizens in general.

The Trubetskoi memorandum's second major point, dealing with the role to be played by the tsar himself, pointedly described the tsar as the logical source of the reforms. It emphasized that the present monarch, like Peter the Great and Alexander II before him, had the glorious challenge and duty to lead his nation and his people, and to reject the false course of either reactionary officials or utopian extremists:

> Before it is too late, let the initiative for this great and holy cause come in this case, too, from the supreme authority. It alone can accomplish [the reforms] in a peaceful manner and thereby solidify all the more the basis of its own strength for future times, for the future of Russia.

Also indicated were the specific steps to be followed by the Emperor.

> It would be beneficial to have an immediate declaration, of principles only, from the height of the throne — in the form of a manifesto or an imperial rescript. In it would be expressed the will of the monarch to abolish the police-bureaucratic system and to assemble for creative work the elective representatives of the land.

The memorandum asked that to ease the transition and to prepare the country, the specific time of convening popular representatives should be indicated in the tsar's declaration. A parallel step would be the formation of an editorial committee, to draft the necessary legislation for consideration by popular representatives. Appointed by the government, this editorial committee would consist of government officials and of public leaders and legal authorities. Its proceedings should be widely reported and freely discussed, so that the press and public organizations would have ample opportunity to comment on the expected transformations. An urgent plea ended the Trubetskoi memorandum:

> A firm expression of the imperial will and the confirmation of an editorial committee with the indicated goal — these alone are the measures which, in our opinion, will most facilitate the calming of the public, and a growing confidence in the state. They will inspire all subjects of the Emperor with a joyful unanimous gratitude and will therefore serve as a valuable and unquestionable guarantee of future regeneration.[27]

IV

Despite, and in part because of, its pleading and patriotic ardor, the Trubetskoi memorandum — along with the main resolution of the third zemstvo congress — set the tone for most public statements except those of the revolutionary extreme. Allowing for changing moods and emphasis, this tone pervaded most zemstvo assemblies[28] and the four national zemstvo congresses that followed in 1905: the fourth in April, the fifth in May, the sixth in June, and the seventh in September.[29] It was also echoed by the national conferences of representatives of municipal self-governments (dumas). These conferences, which by mid-1905 merged with the zemstvo congresses, represented a mixture of wealthy merchants and manufacturers with gentry and intelligentsia owning urban property, and with the lower middle class — the *meshchane*. Here, too, the third zemstvo congress received explicit endorsement, and its theme was echoed.[30] The same affirmation occurred in many of the numerous 1905 gatherings of the national and regional associations of "big business," of leading merchants, manufacturers, and bankers.[31] All of this indicates that during the prologue to the 1905 Revolution Russian liberalism had succeeded in spreading its demands not to the gentry alone but also to the cities and, more specifically, to the previously domant "big business."

Equally interesting was the response of the intelligentsia. At first this took the form of the banquets that the Union of Liberation scheduled to follow soon after the third zemstvo congress. Modeled on the pre-1848 banquets in France, banquets of the intelligentsia honored the fortieth anniversary, on 20 November, 1904, of the Great Reforms in the legal field. As it had done in the case of the zemstvo congress, the government forbade the press to mention these banquets soon after most of them had taken place. And again as with the zemstvo congress, this prohibition did not achieve its purpose, partly because *Pravo* on November 28 published a detailed summary of the banquets. All major cities held these affairs during the two weeks beginning with the November 20–21 weekend. In Moscow some 300 lawyers met separately, and in St. Petersburg, 400. Composed of various segments of the professions — lawyers, professors, journalists, the third element — the main banquets drew more than 650 in Moscow and also in St. Petersburg, 800 in Kiev, and 500 in Odessa. Saratov boasted the largest one, with 1500 attending.

The St. Petersburg banquet was typical. It took place on November 20 in a hotel and was opened by Annenski, populist vice-chairman of the Union of Liberation. Annenski nominated the famous populist writer Korolenko to be chairman. The speakers included Korolenko, the *Pravo* editor Iosif Gessen, and the populist historian V. I. Semevski. The adoption of a resolution climaxed this banquet as it did the others. Peshekhonov, another populist leader of the Union of Liberation, proposed the resolution which was approved unanimously before the banquet adjourned at 2:30 a.m. Mostly prepared in advance by the Union of Liberation, the banquet resolutions did not vary greatly and the St. Petersburg document was typical:

Realized forty years ago and received with general popular sympathy, the court reform had as its aim the establishment of law and legality in Russia. But it did not produce the results expected from it, since through a whole series of further legislative acts and arbitrary administrative orders the very foundations of the reforms were completely distorted. The history of the court statutes shows with particular clarity that under the autocratic-bureaucratic regime which rules the country, the most elementary conditions for a proper civil community cannot be realized, and any partial corrections in the present structure of state institutions do not achieve their goal. Proceeding from these considerations, we, 676 representatives of the intellectual professions of the city of St. Petersburg, have gathered on the day of the fortieth anniversary of the court statutes. We welcome the resolutions of the congress of zemstvo leaders and on our part declare that for a normal development of national life the following, according to our deep conviction, is unquestionably essential:

1. That the following be guaranteed to all citizens of the state as inalienable rights: personal inviolability, freedom of conscience, speech, press, assembly, and association;

2. That all class, national, and religious restrictions be removed and that a real equality of all before the law be established;

3. That all laws be issued and taxes established only with the participation and approval of representatives freely elected by all the people;

4. That through the appropriate organization of ministerial responsibility to the assembly of popular representatives, the lawfulness of all actions and orders of the administrative authorities be assured.

We therefore consider it unquestionably essential that the whole state structure of Russia be reorganized along constitutional principles. Proceeding from this unshakable conviction of ours and taking into consideration the extremely difficult circumstances in which our country finds itself today, we consider it essential that for the realization of the indicated and urgent transformation the following be done:

[1] The immediate convocation of a constituent assembly of freely elected representatives of the entire population of Russia;

[2] Also immediately, before the beginning of the election period, the declaration of a complete and unconditional amnesty for all political and religious crimes;

[3] Appropriate provisions guaranteeing the essential legal conditions for free elections and for the inviolability of the representatives elected.[32]

When the Union of Liberation was planning the November public manifestations, the gentry as well as the intelligentsia had sought to keep their own demonstrations distinct. The banquets were intended to express demands more radical and outspoken than those of the zemstvo congress, as the St. Petersburg banquet resolution clearly indicates with aplomb. These resolutions employed a truculent style clearly designed to impress the intelligentsia and perhaps the lower classes, rather than the tsar and his entourage. And they specifically mentioned a constitution, as the zemstvo resolutions did not. More important, the demand for a constituent assembly, disavowed at the third zemstvo congress even by Petrunkevich, was uppermost at the St. Petersburg banquet. Yet the similarities between the two types of resolution are even more striking than the differences: the banquet resolutions explicitly backed that of the third zemstvo congress and — by implication — its failure to proceed from political to social demands. Thus there was little difference except in tone and in the banquet resolution's appeal for a constitutional assembly. (Even the sweeping demand for amnesty had been foreshadowed in a separate resolution of the third zemstvo congress.) The similarity lies above all in the common insistence that the liberal political reforms were most urgently needed — and must come from the existing regime.

Out of these banquets came novel, now specifically political organizations of professions, which by the end of 1905 ranged from the earlier Group of Zemstvo Constitutionalists on the right to the large, newly founded Peasant Union on the left. Back in December 1904, these new groups had begun to band together in the Union of Unions. Only in mid-1905 did this Union of Unions move decisively to the left of the position of the third zemstvo congress and the banquets. Until then the Union of Unions was headed by Miliukov, who at the time lauded the zemstvo congress resolution as "a beautiful page in our annals" and denied any substantial difference between it and the more radical banquet resolutions.[33]

The still scattered and weak revolutionary organizations opposed and in some instances sought to obstruct the intelligentsia banquets, but these did find an echo even in the labor movement. This echo came from the booming organization of the erratic and antirevolutionary Father Georgi Gapon, the "Assembly of Russian Workers of St. Petersburg." In November 1904, Gapon had been contacted by the "economist" leaders of the Union of Liberation — Kuskova, Bogucharski, Prokopovich. They urged him and several of his worker associates to adopt a resolution similar to the banquet resolutions. At first Gapon's group wavered, but the petition that his mammoth demonstration sought to present to the tsar on Bloody Sunday did bear striking resemblance to the zemstvo and banquet resolutions of November. To be sure, Gapon's bizarre petition was worded in a folksy and religious style, it addressed the emperor as the father of the plain people, and was much more detailed and left in its social and economic demands. Yet in both instances the political demands received priority, and the tsar was identified as the source of the desired transformations.[34]

Thus liberal demands were echoed — temporarily at least — by such divergent groups as "big business" conventions and the workers on Bloody Sunday. The tone varied, the word "constitution" may or may not have been included, and the demands for a constitutional assembly and social reforms were featured here and omitted there.

But the liberal insistence on immediate constitutional reforms, combined with the assumption that they would come
from the tsar, dominated not only the prologue of revolution
but much of 1905. It was not until summer that the polarization so familiar in revolutions decisively splintered the
liberal-shaped consensus.

This book does not delve into the history of the 1905 Revolution itself, a tale well known in outline albeit never yet
told thoroughly. Hence this cannot be the place, either, to
detail the role of liberalism in 1905 — "her joys, her woes,
her highs, her lows." But the epilogue of the revolution, still
more than its prologue, bears out the book's thesis: the
transition of Russian liberalism from gentry to intelligentsia
was completed by 1905. For how different was the Russian
liberalism of 1906 from that of two years earlier. Its central
arena had become the new parliament, the Duma — an
imperfect arena but no more so than the early legislatures
of England, France, Germany. The zemstvo shrank into the
background as much of the gentry reacted to the revolution
and peasant violence by a sharp turn from liberalism (or
apathy) to a pro-government nationalism. At the same time
politically homogeneous parties replaced the earlier coalitions.

Furthermore, in 1906 the new Constitutional Democratic
or Kadet Party represented the liberalism of the intelligentsia and nothing else either to the left or to the right. Most
of the gentry's leading slavophile and moderate liberals
were isolated in a splinter party between the Kadets and
the new "Octobrist" liberals and conservatives. This was
the small Party of Peaceful Regeneration, founded by
Geiden, the slavophile Stakhovich, and the ex-Kadet
Nikolai Ivov. Soon they were joined by disenchanted
Octobrists like Shipov and the ex-Kadet Prince Evgeni

Trubetskoi. Now Shipov and Petrunkevich are no longer the revered leaders of Russian liberalism. Their zemstvo arena gone, the gentry notables give way to mostly younger professionals, a mixture of upper and lower intelligentsia with not a few Jews among them, in contrast to the pre-1905 era: Miliukov, the unchallenged party leader and ideologist; the parliamentarians Muromtsev and Maksim Vinaver; the orators Maklakov and Rodichev; party editors like Gessen and Ganfman; experts such as Mikhail Gertsenshtein, Aleksandr Manuilov, Vladimir Nabokov, and Grigori Iollos; the historians Aleksandr Kornilov and Aleksandr Kizevetter, party lecturers and pamphleteers.

On the left, too, the 1904 coalitions were by 1906 replaced by fragmentation. The *Russkoe bogatstvo* populists considered joining the Socialist Revolutionary party but after its 1906 congress formed instead their own tiny Popular Socialist Party. Of the antiorthodox Marxists, Struve became a spokesman for the right wing of the Kadet Party. Tugan-Baranovski and Bulgakov also joined the Kadets. Remaining Marxists and economists, Kuskova, Prokopovich, Bogucharski, and Khizhniakov united around a magazine entitled "Without Title" (*Bez zaglaviia*). The name is indicative of this group, for it had first failed in preserving the Union of Liberation's St. Petersburg chapter as a continuing organization and then in keeping alive its own new Radical Democratic Party.[35] Like most of the liberals in the gentry, the reform socialists now oscillated — oscillated between the revolutionary parties and the Kadets. So did that portion of the lower intelligentsia which did not join the Kadet Party to become its large, volatile rank and file.

Neither gentry liberalism nor pro-liberal reform socialism were dead. But after 1905, intelligentsia liberalism became more powerful, more widespread, and more influential than either these moderates or the revolutionaries. For a few years at least, Russian liberalism could be equated with the Kadet Party much more than it could have with the liberal intelligentsia of a decade or even two years earlier. This changed whenever the government diminished the relatively free play of politics in the Duma, press, and party life — the quasi-constitutional arena after 1905 that maximized the effectiveness of the Kadet intelligentsia. When such reaction set in, as it did recurrently between 1905 and 1917, the gentry resumed its central role as the element in Russian politics least suspect to the government. Likewise, reform socialists and especially the revolutionaries received more support within the lower intelligentsia whenever government policy stymied the Kadets' semiradical program in the Duma. Yet probably only World War I and the 1917 Revolution shattered the lower intelligentsia's qualified support of liberalism — a support so decisive in contemporary underdeveloped societies where the intelligentsia enjoys a near-monopoly of political *élan* and modernity, and where it is the "outsider" lower intelligentsia that is most willing and able to dynamite existing regimes to attain its Bazarov-like ideals as well as power.* Lenin and Bolshevism are prime examples of the lower intelligentsia, and this fact offers a slighted clue to Soviet ideology, including its anti-liberalism.

V

The half-century between the Great Reforms and the 1905 Revolution form a distinct period in the history of Russian liberalism. More than any other era of Imperial Russia, these decades were marked by industrialization and

---

* In his remarkable book on *The New Class,* Milovan Djilas also argues that what he terms "immature" revolutions require a novel ruling class. Djilas, however, persists in the view that "the social origin of the new class lies in the proletariat;" the evidence both in Eastern Europe and in Asia unmistakably points to the lower intelligentsia.

agricultural crisis. In the zemstvo the Great Reforms had created for liberals a new arena which retained its central role up to the end of the period. During this period, too, the newness, the weakness, and the amorphousness of both liberals and revolutionaries made the relationship between them hazy and politically unimportant. And together the Great Reforms and industrialization spawned the new professional middle class, the "grandsons" of the intelligentsia, which reached political maturity by the turn of the twentieth century.

For a concluding assessment of this period, one may fruitfully compare the Russian varieties of liberal experience. The contrast between the liberalism of the gentry and that of the later intelligentsia appears in their thoroughly different history, temperament, and style of life. The gentry liberals, a small group of financially independent notables, ventured into reformist and philanthropic activities from their often still profitable and leisurely rural existence and the traditional privileges of their class. The intelligentsia, on the other hand, was committed to wholly modern and still novel occupations in a society only half modernizing.

This gulf between styles of life of gentry and intelligentsia explains their different approach to "small deeds" and "senseless dreams," to lesser and tangible improvements as against seemingly more remote and grandiose reforms. Upon its ascendancy in the 1890's and after, the intelligentsia sought actively and without hesitation to replace the gentry's local and mainly cultural small deeds with its own senseless dreams. These were to be national and to aim at nothing less than its twin objectives, constitution and democracy. But as Russian liberalism changed from a cluster of ideals and local activism to an organized national movement, the liberal intelligentsia found itself stymied by a profound tactical problem.

Eager as it was to replace the gentry's small deeds with its own senseless dreams, it continued to need the gentry very badly. Reforms from above, from the *ancien régime*, were the only alternative to revolution — and within a non-revolutionary, static situation the voice of the gentry had far more impact on officialdom, court, and tsar than that of lower intelligentsia or the masses. Likewise, until the demanded parliament was granted, the vast and gentry-dominated zemstvo structure of rural self-government offered a base of operations preferable to any other in the country. This explains the years of tactical wavering by the otherwise determined intelligentsia majority in the Union of Liberation. It also explains why the intelligentsia continued to conciliate the liberal but nonconstitutionalist and nondemocratic elements of the gentry as it would hardly have done otherwise.

Like the liberalism of the gentry, that of the intelligentsia was formed in years exceptional for Russian autocracy. The gentry liberals emerged "on the eve" — amidst the heady, rosy expectations of the Great Reforms, with government prestige and controls temporarily weakened by a disastrous war and change of monarchs. It took them several years and even longer to scale down their own erstwhile "senseless dreams" to the prosaic small deeds of the later nineteenth century. The same pattern recurred with the liberal intelligentsia. Taking shape in the prerevolutionary years of the early century and during 1905 itself, intelligentsia liberalism started with a similar optimism and insistence on its "senseless dreams." But as the revolutionary wave receded, so did this liberal optimism. Most of the dozen years between 1905 and 1917 were devoted to small deeds not unlike those proposed by the gentry. The arena alone had changed from zemstvo to Duma. Legalized political parties and a freer press made the new small deeds fit the intelligentsia's ideals and temperament more than the gentry's small deeds ever could.

To what extent, then, did these Russian varieties of liberalism really differ? In retrospect some of the outstanding Russian liberals of the day, notably Maklakov and also Tyrkova-Williams, have traced much of their country's woes to what they labeled the dogmatism and intransigence of intelligentsia liberalism, as distinguished from the gentry's pragmatism and moderation. Certainly some statements of Petrunkevich, Miliukov, and Struve seem to support this view, as does the whole radical mystique of the "liberation movement." But doubt is raised by the similar ebb and flow of the gentry's and intelligentsia's senseless dreams and small deeds. Thus the gentry liberals, too, had their strident and unrealistic moments, as did much of early (and later) Western liberalism. Even if the Maklakov type of criticism is factually valid, it may be neglecting the historical context. All movements tend to be quite flexible and empirical in matters of current relevance to them, as illustrated notably by Lenin's (and Stalin's) theoretical and tactical dexterity. Dogmatism and intransigence characterize periods and aspects where a movement has few or no prospects of immediate success. It is in such situations that one may well apply to intelligentsia liberalism, too, Joseph Schumpeter's notion of the radicalism of impotence.

In fact, the similarities in the liberalism of gentry and of intelligentsia were strikingly great. Both lacked an elaborate formal ideology, a theory of ethics, politics, or economics. Both derived much of their *élan* from the uncomplicated westernizing ideals of the mid-century, but neither gave Western models and precedents overriding emphasis. Both rejected revolution as a means of attaining their goals, and both talked in terms of specific changes rather than a total seizure of power and a total metamorphosis of society. In important ways, then, the similarities between Russian liberals in the gentry and those in the intelligentsia were greater than the differences. The similarities were not to be found in the long-run aims. Life situation, temperament, ideology, and circumstances all made these ends unmistakably diverge. It was rather in the means they favored that the two varieties of liberalism were surprisingly alike. A common dilemma and a common environment made both act similarly and feel analogous tactical doubts and frustrations. Zemstvo gentry and Kadet intelligentsia confronted the same central liberal dilemma — the dilemma of attaining complex, specifically Western objectives in an illiberal, underdeveloped society. Were the only alternatives those of conciliating the illiberal government or changing it by illiberal means? Or could a third choice be found or made? On each occasion, the range of plausible liberal answers was narrowly circumscribed by the same environment, the same Russia. This Russia was still a largely pastoral society, half welcoming and half repulsing modernization. Islands of the latest culture and technology grew steadily but tortuously and unevenly in a sea of medieval and feudal backwardness. And government chicanery and suppression coexisted with a most untotalitarian leeway for oppositional thought and activity.

Could such an underdeveloped society provide a satisfactory solution to the liberal dilemma? Of the Russian varieties of liberal experience, the zemstvo gentry and the Kadet intelligentsia both failed. Yet Russia's liberal dilemma was not unique. In the past century or more, the story of Russia has been the story also of eastern Europe, of Latin Europe and America, of China and Japan, even of Germany and France. All of these early underdeveloped societies lunged and dipped and convulsed. Most were centuries and worlds removed from the advanced nation-states on the northern shores of the Atlantic, from the few which approximate the ideal type of the West: the gradual, consistent molding of a modern and free society. All underdeveloped societies have had to wrestle with the same liberal dilemma; the odds against liberalism were no less and no more in Russia.

SOURCES

Unlike Russia's revolutionaries, with their intelligentsia forerunners and Bolshevik heirs, Russian liberals have received little attention from historians — even less attention than the also slighted *ancien régime* and its supporters. As the Bibliography below indicates, in Russia a good deal was actually published on the country's liberalism between the Great Reforms and the 1905 Revolution. But in no language has there been a synthesis or a bibliography, and the sources remain uneven and scattered.

My attempt to fill this gap was facilitated by bountiful assistance from the following:

The accessible key survivors, almost all octogenarians in 1950 when they submitted to exhaustive interviews in Western Europe: Semeon Frank, Ekaterina Kuskova, Vasili Maklakov, Vladimir Obolenski, Sergei Prokopovich, Ariadna Tyrkova-Williams.

My teachers, Selig Perlman at the University of Wisconsin and Michael Karpovich at Harvard; that unique research cicerone, Boris I. Nicolaevsky; my friends, Paul W. Massing, Edward A. Shils, and Sir Isaiah Berlin; and this book's editor, Ellen Siegelman.

Harvard University, and in particular the Society of Fellows (research fellowship, 1949–1953), and the Russian Research Center (technical assistance since 1948).

Bibliotheque de Documentation Internationale Contemporaine of the University of Paris, the Slavic Library of Helsinki University, Columbia's Archive of Russian and East European History and Culture, and especially the Boris I. Nicolaevsky Collection in New York and Harvard University Library.

The Lowell Institute of Boston, which invited me to deliver the Lowell Lectures for March, 1953, that formed the first draft of this book.

Brandeis University, and my students and colleagues there since 1953.

Principal Sources

On Russian liberalism in the later nineteenth century, the most authoritative source is the third volume of the massively detailed and documented *Istoriia zemstva* by Veselovski. On the early twentieth century it is the lengthy essay, "Soiuz osvobozhdeniia," by Shakhovskoi, who was not only a leader of later Russian liberalism but also its historian. These works are best augmented by some post-1917 autobiographies and also by two briefer and less documented pre-1917 descriptions: Belokonski's *Zemskoe dvizhenie* and Finance Minister Witte's much-discussed *Samoderzhavie i zemstvo*. Very useful is the partly autobiographical "Who's Who" in the volume *Rússkie vedomosti, 1863–1913*.

The pre-1917 descriptions portray earlier antigovernment activities with striking gusto and detail. Of the remaining gaps, many — far from all — are filled by various leaders' post-1917 reminiscences, although most were written by uprooted émigrés lacking their old records and their old vigor. The earlier book-length life stories of Astrov, Berdiaev, Bulgakov, Gessen, Kizevetter, Georgi Lvov, Petrunkevich, Shipov, and Evgeni Trubetskoi have been augmented by those issued in the 1950's by Chekhov Publishing House (Buryshkin, Maklakov, Miliukov, Struve, Sergei Trubetskoi, and Tyrkova-Williams) and a few incomplete autobiographies (Kuskova, Obolenski, Rodichev, and Struve).

The most extensive survey of the turn of the twentieth century is *Obshchestvennoe dvizhenie v Rossii v nachale XX-go veka*. This is a mammoth post-1905 collective work by leading Mensheviks. The fact that the authors are all *éngagés* ideologically qualifies but far from nullifies the four volumes' usefulness. The same may be said of the one major Soviet work on this book's topic, Chermenski's

Burzhuaziia i tsarizm v revoliutsii 1905–1907 gg. Two ambitious Soviet reference works, *Pervaia russkaia revoliutsiia* and Mezer's *Slovarnyi ukazatel po knigovedeniiu,* are invaluable. So is the sole outstanding analytical study of the subject, published by a noted German scholar in a book-length essay as early as 1906: Max Weber, "Zur Lage der bürgerlichen Demokratie in Russland."

Only recently three American studies have touched upon the subject of this book: Raeff's new and as yet unpublished interpretation in "The Peasant Commune in the Political Thinking of Russian Publicists, Laissez-faire Liberalism in the Reign of Alexander II," several essays in his pupils' *Festschrift* to Professor Karpovich (*Russian Thought and Politics*), and Karpovich's own article, "Two Types of Russian Liberalism: Maklakov and Miliukov." A different American contribution has come from the Ford Foundation-sponsored Chekhov Publishing House in New York. This contribution took the form of the six important biographies, in Russian, already listed.

Bibliography

Agrarnyi vopros, kn. P. D. Dolgorukov and I. I. Petrunkevich, ed. (Moscow, vol. I, 1905, vol. II, 1906). The first volume reproduces the speeches and deliberations of a special conference on the agricultural problem, sponsored by the Group of Zemstvo Constitutionalists on 28–29 April 1905 in Moscow.

ANNENSKI, N. F. A. Annenskaia, "Iz proshlykh let, vospominaniia o N. F. Annenskom," *Russkoe bogatstvo* (St. Petersburg), January 1913, February 1913, and July 1913.

N. F. Annenski, vospominaniia o nem, V. G. Korolenko and others, ed. (St. Petersburg, 1914).

A. P., *Samoderzhavie, biurokratiia i zemstvo* (Berlin, 1902).

Aptekman, O. V., "Partiia 'Narodnogo prava', po lichnym vospominaniiam," *Byloe* (St. Petersburg), July 1907.

Astrov, N. I., *Vospominaniia* (Paris, 1941).

Belokonski, I. P., *Zemskoe dvizhenie* (2nd ed., Moscow, 1914). First edition, in 1910, also entitled *Zemstvo i konstitutsiia.*

Berdiaev, Nikolai, *Samopoznanie, opyt filosofskoi avtobiografii* (Paris, 1949).

——— *Subekitivizm i individualizm v obshchestvennoi filosofii* (St. Petersburg, 1901).

——— *Sub specie aeternitatis (1900–1906 g.)* (St. Petersburg, 1907). See also *Problemy idealizma.*

Bogdanovich, A. I., *Nasushchnyi vopros* (London, 1895). People's Rights Party pamphlet published with Mikhailovski approval.

Bogucharski [Iakovlev], V. Ia., *Iz istorii politicheskoi borby v 70-kh i 80-kh gg. XIX veka* (Moscow, 1912).

——— "Zemski Soiuz' kontsa 70-kh i nachala 80-kh godov XIX veka," in *Iubileinyi zemski sbornik* (listed separately).

[Bogucharski, V.], Editorial Note in *Istoricheskii sbornik "Nasha strana"* (St. Petersburg, 1907), pp. 28–30, footnote, and 36, footnote. On the Union of Liberation in 1904.

―――― in Belokonski, *Zemskoe dvizhenie* (listed separately), pp. 92–93. On the founding of *Osvobozhdenie* and the Union of Liberation.

Budberg, baron R. Iu., "Iz vospominanii uchastnika zemskikh sezdov," *Minuvshie gody* (St. Petersburg), January 1908.

―――― "Sezd zemskikh deiatelei 6–9 noiabria 1904 goda v Peterburge, po lichnym vospominaniiam," *Byloe* (St. Petersburg), March 1907.

Bulgakov, S. N., *Avtobiograficheskie zametki* (Paris, 1946). Emphasis is on Russian Orthodox religious mysticism, of which Bulgakov — like Berdiaev — became a foremost theorist soon after 1905.

―――― *Kapitalizm i zemledelie* (2 vols., St. Petersburg, 1900).

―――― *Ot marksizma k idealizmu*, 1896–1903 (St. Petersburg, 1903). See also *Problemy idealizma*, and Zander, *Bog i mir*.

Burtsev, VI., *Za sto let (1800–1896)* (London, 1897). Part One contains documents of Russian opposition movements and Part Two a chronology.

Buryshkin, P. A., *Moskva kupecheskaia* (New York, 1954).

Chastnoe soveshchanie gorodskikh deiatelei 15–16–20 iunia 1905 goda (Moscow, 1909). Also records preceding conferences and subsequent local statements.

Chastnoe soveshchanie zemskikh deiatelei proiskhodivshee 6, 7, 8 i 9 noiabria 1904 goda v S.-Peterburge (Moscow, 1905).

Chermenski, E. D., *Burzhuaziia i tsarism v revoliutsii 1905–1907 gg.* (Moscow, 1939). Refers to unpublished documents in Soviet archives.

Chernenkov, N. N., *Agrarnaia programma partii narodnoi svobody i ee posleduiushchaia razrabotka* (St. Petersburg, 1907). Written by one of the Kadet Party's leaders, it discusses both Kadet links to the Union of Liberation program and the April 1905 conference of the Group of Zemstvo Constitutionalists (see *Agrarnyi vopros*).

Chicherin, B. N., *Neskolko sovremennykh voprosov* (Moscow, 1862).

―――― *O narodnom predstavitelstve* (Moscow, 1866).

―――― *Zemstvo i moskovskaia duma* (vol. IV of his *Vospominaniia*, Moscow, 1934).

[Chicherin, B. N.], "Russkii patriot" (pseudonym), *Rossiia nakanune XX stoletiia* (Berlin, 1900).

Chuprov, A. I., *Rechi i stati* (3 vols., Moscow, 1909).

[Chuprov, A. I., and others], *Vliianie urozhaev i khlebnykh tsen na raznye storony ekonomicheskoi zhizni, doklad prof. A. I. Chuprova i preniia v III otdelenii Imperatorskogo volnogo ekonomicheskogo obshchestva* (St. Petersburg, 1897).

CONSTITUTIONAL DEMOCRATIC [KADET] PARTY (Partiia narodnoi svobody). *Otchet tsentralnogo komiteta konstitutsionno-demokraticheskoi partii za dva goda, s 18 oktiabria 1905 g. po oktiabr 1907 g.* (St. Petersburg, 1907).
Sezd 12–18 oktiabria 1905 g. (St. Petersburg, 1905). Official report on first congress.
Zakonodatelnye proekty i predpolozheniia partii Narodnoi svobody, 1905–1907 gg. N. I. Astrov, F. F. Kokoshkin, S. A. Muromtsev, P. I. Novgorodtsev, and D. I. Shakhovskoi, ed. (St. Petersburg, 1907).
See also Chernenkov, *Agrarnaia programma*.

Debogori-Mokrievich, VI., *Vospominaniia* (vol. I, Paris, 1894).

Doklad komissii Moskovskogo universiteta 1901 goda o prichinakh studencheskikh volnenii (vol. II of *Osvobozhdenie's Materialy po universitetskomu voprosu*, Paris, 1904).

"Doklad Ratseva ot 9/22 oktiabria 1904 g., za No. 282," published in *Russkii politicheskii sysk za granitsei*, L. P. Menshikov, ed. (Paris, 1914). Police report on the Paris conference of Russian oppositional groups.

Dolgorukov, kn. Pavel D., "Avtobiografiia," in *Russkie vedomosti, 1863–1913* (listed separately), Part Two, pp. 63–64.

Dolgorukov, kn. Petr, "Pamiati gr. P. A. Geiden," *Byloe* (St. Petersburg), August 1907.

Dragomanov, M. P., "Avtobiografiia," *Byloe* (St. Petersburg, June 1906).

———— *Liberalizm i zemstvo v Rossii, 1858–1883* (Geneva, 1889).

———— *Politicheskie sochineniia* (Moscow, 1908). Contains biographical essay by Bogdan Kistiakovski.

———— *Sobranie politicheskikh sochinenii i statei* (Paris, vol. I, 1905, vol. II, 1906).
See also Kistiakovski, "Dragomanov."

Dzhanshiev, G. A., *A. M. Unkovski* (Moscow, 1894).

FRANK, S. *Sbornik pamiati S. L. Franka*, Vasili Zenkovski, ed. (Munich, 1954). Includes Frank bibliography by L. A. Zander.

Frank, S., *Biografia P. B. Struve* (New York, 1956). Personal recollections of Struve and an epilogue on his ("conservative liberal") thought.
See also *Problemy idealizma.*

Ganfman, M., "Pervye mesiatsy, iz vospominanii," *Rech* (Petrograd), 23 February 1916.

Gapon, G., *Istoriia moei zhizni* (Leningrad, 1925). This edition is richly annotated.

Geiden, graf P. A., Autobiographical essay and letters, in volume commemorating his death, *Trudy Imperatorskogo volnogo ekonomicheskogo obshchestva* (St. Petersburg), November-December 1907.
See also kn. Petr Dolgorukov, "Pamiati gr. P. A. Geiden."

Gessen, I. V., *V dvukh vekakh* (Berlin, 1937).

Gessen, I. V., and A. I. Kaminka, *Konstitutsionnoe gosudarstvo* (St. Petersburg, 1905). Published by *Pravo.*

Gessen, V. M., *Na rubezhe, 1901–1905* (St. Petersburg, 1906).

Golovin, F. A., "Iz zapisok F. A. Golovina: S. A. Muromtsev," *Krasnyi arkhiv* (Moscow), 1933, no. 58.

Goltsev, V. A., "Iz vospominanii i perepiski," *Russkaia mysl* (Moscow), April 1905.
See also *Pamiati Goltseva.*

IMPERIAL FREE ECONOMIC SOCIETY. A. N. Beketov, *Istoricheskii ocherk dvadtsatipiatiletiia deiatelnosti Imperatorskogo volnogo ekonomicheskogo obshchestva s 1865 do 1890 goda* (St. Petersburg, 1890).
 I. Sh. V., *Trudy Imperatorskogo volnogo ekonomicheskogo obshchestva za poslednie 15 let izdaniia (gody 1889–1903), ukazatel* (St. Petersburg, 1904).
 A. I. Khodnev, *Istoriia Imperatorskogo volnogo ekonomicheskogo Obshchestva s 1765 do 1865 g.* (St. Petersburg, 1865).

Imperial Free Economic Society, "Iz del komissii po peresmotru ustava I. v. e. obshchestva v 1900 g.," *Trudy* (St. Petersburg), November-December 1904.

―――― "K istorii I. v. e. obshchestva, kopii dokumentov 1894–1906 gg.," *Trudy* (St. Petersburg), July-October 1906, November-December 1906, and January-June 1907.

―――― *Otchet o deistviiakh za 1899 god* (St. Petersburg, 1900). Membership list as of 1 January, 1900, on pp. 123–147.

Intelligentsiia v Rossii (St. Petersburg, 1910). Miliukov, Petrunkevich, Tugan-Baranovski and others reply to *Vekhi.*

Iordanski, N. I., *Konstitutsionnoe dvizhenie 60-kh godov* (St. Petersburg, 1906).

Iubileinyi sbornik Literaturnogo fonda (St. Petersburg, 1909). Includes Kornilov, *Piatidesiatiletie* (listed separately).

Iubileinyi zemskii shornik, 1864–1914, B. B. Veselovski and Z. G. Frenkel, ed. (St. Petersburg, 1914).

Ivanovich, V., *Rossiiskie partii, soiuzy i ligi* (St. Petersburg, 1906).

Izvlecheniia iz knigi A. I. Georgievskogo: "Kratkii ocherk pravitelstvennykh mer i prednachertanii protiv studencheskikh bezporiadkov" (vol. I of *Osvobozhdenie's Materialy po universitetskomu voprosu,* Stuttgart, 1902).

"Kadety v 1905–1906 gg.," *Kransyi arkhiv* (Moscow), 1931, No. 46 and 47–48. Minutes of Kadet executive committee.

[Kamenev, L. B.] Iu. K. (pseudonym) *Sotsial-demokraticheskie izdaniia [za granitsei]* (Paris, 1913). Comparative chronology and bibliography of orthodox-economist controversy, pp. 7–13.

Karpovich, Michael, "Two Types of Russian Liberalism: Maklakov and Miliukov," in *Continuity and Change in Russian and Soviet Thought,* Ernest J. Simmons, ed. (Cambridge, 1955).

———— "Kommentarii: 1905 god," *Novyi zhurnal* (New York), 1955, no. 43.

Kennan, George, "The Last Appeal of the Russian Liberals," *Century Magazine* (New York), vol. 35, no. 1 (November 1887).

Khizhniakov, V. M., *Vospominaniia zemskogo deiatelia* (Petrograd, 1916).

Khizhniakov, V. V., "Avtobiografiia," in *Russkie vedomosti, 1863–1913* (listed separately), Part Two, pp. 188–189.

[Kirpichnikov, S. D.] S. D. K. (pseudonym), *Soiuz soiuzov* (St. Petersburg, 1906).

Kistiakovski, B., "M. P. Dragomanov po ego pismam," *Russkaia mysl* (Moscow, September 1911).

———— *Stranitsy proshlogo* (Moscow, 1912). Polemic against Bogucharski on Russian liberalism in the late 1870's.
See also *Problemy idealizma.*

Kizevetter, A. A., *Na rubezhe dvukh stoletii* (Prague, 1929).

———— "Zemskii soiuz ili Sviashchennaia druzhina?" *Russkie vedomosti* (Moscow), 22 April 1912.

Kokoshkin, F. F., "Avtobiografiia," in *Russkie vedomosti, 1863–1913* (listed separately), Part Two, pp. 86–90.

———— *O pravakh natsionalnostei i detsentralizatsii, doklad biuro sezdu zemskikh i gorodskikh deiatelei 12–15 sent. 1905 goda i postanovleniia sezda* (Moscow, 1906). The nationality question became prominent and controversial only in mid-1905.

Koliupanov, *Biografiia Aleksandra Ivanovicha Kosheleva* (Moscow, vol. I, in two books, 1889, vol. II, 1892).

Kornilov, A. A., "K istorii konstitutsionnogo dvizheniia kontsa 70-kh i nachala 80-kh godov," *Russkaia mysl* (Moscow), July 1913.

———— *Obshchestvennoe dvizhenie pri Aleksandre II* (Moscow, 1909).

———— *Piatidesiatilietie Literaturnogo fonda, 1859–1909* (St. Petersburg, 1909).

———— *Semeistvo Bakuninykh,* vol. I: *Molodye gody Mikhaila Bakunina* (Moscow, 1915).

———— Detailed criticism of vols. I and II of Veselovski, *Istoriia zemstva* (listed separately), in *Izvestiia S.-Petersburgskogo politekhnicheskogo instituta* (St. Petersburg), 1910, no. 14.

Korolenko, V. G., *Pisma, 1881–1921* (Petrograd, 1922).

———— Letters by Korolenko to Gorki, quoted in *Letopis revoliutsii* (Berlin), 1923, no. 1, p. 43, and in Maksim Gorki, *Sobranie sochinenii* (vol. XXII of 2nd ed., Moscow, 1933), p. 130.

Korsh, V. F., *Etiudy* (St. Petersburg, 1884). Includes biography.

Koshelev, A. I., *Konstitutsiia, samoderzhavie i zemskaia duma* (Leipzig, 1862).

———— *Nashe polozhenie* (Berlin, 1875).

———— *Zapiski, 1821–1883 gody* (Berlin, 1884).
    See also Koliupanov, *Biografiia.*

Krestianskii stroi, kn. P. D. Dolgorukov and graf S. L. Tolstoi, ed. (St. Petersburg, 1905).

Kuskova, E. D., "Davno minuvshee," *Novyi zhurnal* (New York), 1955, no. 43, to 1957, no. 48. Personal reminiscences of the 1870's and 1880's.

———— "Kren nalevo, iz proshlogo," *Sovremennye zapiski* (Paris), 1930, no. 44.

———— "Nadpole i podpole marksizma," *Novoe russkoe slovo* (New York), 23 July 1954 and 24 July 1954.

———— "Otvet na vopros — kto my?" *Bez zaglaviia* (St. Petersburg), 1906, no. 3.

—— "Zigzagi pamiati," *Novoe russkoe slovo* (New York), 17 July 1952 and 18 July 1952.

—— partly autobiographical essay-review in *Byloe* (St. Petersburg), October 1906. The inception and publication of the "Credo" are described on pp. 324–326, footnote.

[Kuskova, E. D.], "Credo," English translation in V. I. Lenin, *Selected Works* (vol I, New York [1935]), pp. 516–519.

—— "Pisma E. D. Kuskovoi 'Timofeiu' (Ts. Kopelzonu-Grishinu)," *Proletarskaia revoliutsiia* (Moscow), March 1928.

—— M. M. (pseudonym), "Pismo k Akselrodu" (1898), in G. V. Plekhanov, *Sochineniia* (vol. XII, Moscow [1924]), pp. 487–494.

—— *Son pod 1-oe maia* (Geneva, 1898).

—— *Stachka lzhi* (Geneva, 1898).

Kuzmin-Karavaev, V. D., *Iz epokhi osvoboditelnogo dvizheniia, do 17 oktiabria 1905 goda* (*Sbornik statei*) (St. Petersburg, 1907).

Leontowitsch, Victor, *Geschichte des Liberalismus in Russland* [1762–1917] (Frankfurt, 1957). Surveys liberal tendencies in Russia's government and thought.

Libanov, G. M., *Studencheskoe dvizhenie 1899 g., s dokumentalnymi prilozheniiami*, vol. 28 of Russian Free Press Fund (London, 1901).

Loi fundamentale de l'Empire Russe (Paris, 1905). Translation of *Osnovnoi gosudarstvennyi zakon Rossiiskoi imperii* (listed separately), both published by *Osvobozhdenie*.

Maklakov, V. A., *Iz vospominanii* (New York, 1954).

—— *Vlast i obshchestvennost na zakate staroi Rossii* (3 vols., Paris [1936]).

Melkaia zemskaia edinitsa, kn. P. D. Dolgorukov and kn. D. I. Shakhovskoi, ed. (2 vols., St. Petersburg, 1902).

Mezer, A. V., *Slovarnyi ukazatel po knigovedeniiu* (2nd ed., vol. I, Moscow, 1931), sections "Gazety" and "Zhurnaly."

Miakotin, V. A., *Iz istorii russkogo obshchestva* (St. Petersburg, 1902).

—— "O narodno-sotsialisticheskoi partii," *Narodno-sotsialisticheskoe obozrenie* (St. Petersburg), 1906, no. 1.

Mikhailovski, K. N., *Sobranie sochinenii* (3rd ed., 10 vols., St. Petersburg, 1909). Bibliography in tenth volume and also in *Russkoe bogatstvo, Ukazatel statei* (listed separately).

Miliukov, P. N., *Glavnye techeniia russkoi istoricheskoi mysli* (Moscow, 1897).

—— *Gosudarstvennoe khoziaistvo Rossii v pervoi chetverti XVIII stoletiia i reforma Petra Velikogo* (St. Petersburg, 1892).

—— *Iz istorii russkoi intelligentsii* (St. Petersburg, 1902).

—— *Ocherki po istorii russkoi kultury* (St. Petersburg, vol. I, 1896, vol. II, 1897, vol. III, 1901. "Jubilee edition," 3 vols., Paris, 1930–1937).

—— "Rokovye gody. Iz vospominanii [1904–1906]," *Russkie Zapiski* (Paris), installments from April 1938 to August-September 1939 (nos. 4–21).

—— [Milyoukov, Paul] *Russia and its Crisis* (Chicago, 1906).

—— *Spornye voprosy finansovoi istorii Moskovskogo gosudarstva* (St. Petersburg, 1892).

—— *Vospominaniia 1859–1917* (2 vols., New York, 1955). First volume covers up to 1907.

—— Annual surveys of Russian literature (and history), in *Athenaeum* (London), 6 July 1889, 5 July 1890, 4 July 1891, 2 July 1892, 1 July 1893, 7 July 1894, 6 July 1895, 4 July 1896. See also *P. N. Miliukov, 1859–1929.*

[Miliukov, P. N.] *cc* (pseudonym), articles in *Osvobozhdenie*:
No. 11 (18 November 1902), "Chto takoe 'konstitutsiia' Loris-Melikova?"
No. 17 (16 February 1903), "K ocherednym voprosam."
No. 19 (19 March 1903), "Derzhavnyi maskarad."
No. 43 (7 March 1904), "Voina i russkaia oppozitsiia."
No. 45 (2 April 1904), "Voina i russkaia oppozitsiia."
No. 52 (19 July 1904), "Ocherednye zadachi russkikh konstitutsionalistov."
No. 57 (2 October 1904), "Novyi kurs."
No. 60 (10 November 1904), "Fiasko 'novogo kursa'."
No. 74 (13 July 1905), "Rossiia organizuetsia."
No. 74 (13 July 1905), " 'Soiuz osvobozhdeniia' i drugie politicheskie partii."
No. 75 (6 August 1905), "Itti ili ne itti v Gosudarstvennuiu dumu?"

Mirnyi, S. [Kn. D. I. Shakhovskoi], *Adresa zemstv, 1894–1895, i ikh politicheskaia programma* (Geneva, 1895).

Muromtsev, S. A., "Moskovskoe iuridicheskoe obshchestvo za istekshee dvadtsatipiatiletie" (1888), in vol. II of his *Stati i rechi.*

—— "Pisma iz Moskvy" (1881 and 1885), in vol. III of his *Stati i rechi.*

—— *Stati i rechi* (5 vols., Moscow, 1910).

See also Golovin, "Iz zapisok," and *Sergei Andreevich Muromtsev*, which includes a biography by Miliukov and a bibliography.

[Muromtsev and others], *Proekt osnovnogo zakono Rossiiskoi imperii* (listed separately).

—— *V pervye dni ministerstva gr. M. T. Loris-Melikova* (Berlin, 1881). The first publication of the 1880 constitutionalist memorandum. The memorandum was translated into English by the older George Kennan (see his "The Last Appeal of the Russian Liberals," listed separately, pp. 56–63).

[Nevski, V.] V. N. (pseudonym), "Bibliografiia o zubatovskikh soiuzakh, 'legalnykh rabochikh soiuzakh', Gapone, i 9-om ianvare," *Krasnaia letopis* (Petrograd), 1922, no. 1.

Nicolaevsky, B. I., "P. B. Struve, 1870–1944," *Novyi zhurnal* (New York), 1950, no. 10. The foremost specialist on Russian revolutionary movements analyzes the young Struve's relation to Marxism.

Nuzhdy derevni, po rabotam komitetov o nuzhdakh selskokhoziaistvennoi promyshlennosti, N. N. Lvov and A. A. Stakhovich, ed. (2 vols., St. Petersburg, 1904).

Obolenski, V. A., *Ocherki minuvshego, obrazy iz moego detstva* (Belgrad, 1931).

Obshchestvennoe dvizhenie v Rossii v nachale XX-go veka, L. Martov, P. Maslov, and A. Potresov, ed. (4 vols., St. Petersburg, 1909–1911).

Obshchii svod po imperii rezultatov razrabotki dannykh pervoi vseobshchei perepisi naseleniia, proizvedennoi 28 ianvaria 1897 goda, N. A. Troinitski, ed. (2 vols., St. Petersburg, 1905).

"Old Zemstvo Men" [Starye Zemtsy], 1901 open letter. Text in V. I. Lenin, *Sochineniia*, vol. V (3rd ed., Moscow, 1934), pp. 74–78. Originally published in *Iskra* [Munich], 10 March 1902 (no. 18) and (with minor variations) in *Revoliutsionnaia Rossiia* [Geneva], February 1902 (no. 1).

Osnovnoi gosudarstvennyi zakon Rossiiskoi imperii, vyrabotannyi gruppoi chlenov 'Soiuza Osvobozhdeniia' (vol. I of *Osvobozhdenie*'s *Materialy po vyrabotke russkoi konstitutsii*, Paris, 1905).

OSVOBOZHDENIE.

(1) *Osvobozhdenie*, semimonthly magazine.
   Stuttgart: nos. 1 (18 June 1902) to 56 (7 September 1904).
   Paris: nos. 57 (2 October 1904) to 78–79 (5 October 1905).

(2) *Osvobozhdenie*, book-form collections of articles.
Osvobozhdenie, Book One (Stuttgart, 1903), and Book Two (Paris, 1904).

(3) *Listok Osvobozhdeniia* (special bulletins).
Stuttgart: nos. 1 (15 April 1904) to 16 (25 August 1904).
Paris: nos. 17 (19 November 1904) to 26 (7 March 1905).
The *Listok* was a special bulletin, two to four pages long, which appeared at irregular intervals (between a week and a month). It was intended for quicker and wider distribution than *Osvobozhdenie*.

(4) *Osvobozhdenie*, pamphlet series.
(a) Stuttgart, 1902: *Russkii zakon i rabochii, sostavlennaia v otdele promyshlennosti ministerstva finansov zapiska o peresmotra statei zakona, karaiushchikh zabastovki i dosrochnye rastorzheniia dogovorov o naime, i o zhelatelnosti ustanovleniia organizatsii rabochikh v tseliakh samopomoshchi* (vol. I of *Osvobozhdenie's Materialy po rabochemu voprosu*).
Izvlecheniia iz knigi A. I. Georgievskogo (listed separately).

(b) Stuttgart, 1903: *Zakonodatelnye materialy o starostakh v promyshlennykh predpriatiiakh* (vol. II of *Osvobozhdenie's Materialy po rabochemu voprosu*).
Ministr finansov i Gosudarstvennyi sovet o finansovom polozhenii Rossii, zhurnal obshchego sobraniia Gosudarstvennogo soveta 30 dekabria 1902 g.
Doklad voronezhskogo uezdnogo komiteta o nuzhdakh selsko-khoziaistvennoi promyshlennosti.
Kishinevskii pogrom.
Osvobozhdenie, Book One (listed under (2) above).

(c) Stuttgart, 1904: *Delo o t. n. boevoi organizatsii, obvinitelnyi akt.*
Doklad komissii Moskovskogo universiteta (listed separately).

(d) Paris, 1904: *Usilenie gubernatorskoi vlasti, proekt f.-Pleve.*
Osvobozhdenie, Book Two (listed under (2) above).

(e) Paris, 1905: *Zemskii sezd 6-go i sl. noiabria 1904 g., kratkii otchet.*
Zemstvo i politicheskaia svoboda, zhurnaly sobraniia-komissii saratovskogo gubernatorskogo zemstva (1905 g.).
Obshchestvennoe dvizhenie pri Aleksandre II [by A. A. Kornilov] (1909 edition listed under Kornilov).

Osnovnoi gosudarstvennyi zakon Rossiiskoi imperii (listed separately).

Loi fundamentale de l'Empire Russe (listed separately).

Proekt osnovnogo zakona Rossiiskoi imperii (listed separately).

Dragomanov, *Sobranie politicheskikh sochinenii*, vol. I (listed separately).

(f) Paris, 1906: *Proekt osnovnogo gosudarstvennogo zakona Rossiiskoi imperii, sostavlen odnim finliandskim politicheskim deiatelem* (vol. III of *Osvobozhdenie*'s *Materialy po vyrabotke russkoi konstitutsii*).

Dragomanov, *Sobranie politicheskikh sochinenii*, vol. II (listed separately).

Otchet o deiatelnosti byvshego S.-Peterburgskogo komiteta gramotnosti Imperatorskogo volnogo ekonomicheskogo obshchestva za 1895 god (St. Petersburg, 1896).

Otchet po oblastnoi selskokhoziaistvennoi i kulturno-prosvetitelnoi vystavka severnogo kraia 1903 goda (Iaroslavl, 1903).

Pamiati Viktora Aleksandrovicha Goltseva, A. A. Kizevetter, ed. (Moscow, 1910).

Panina, gr. S. V., "Na peterburgskoi okraine," *Novyi zhurnal* (New York), 1957, no. 48. Reminiscences about mass education by the stepdaughter of Petrunkevich.

Partiia mirnogo obnovleniia, ee obrazovanie i deiatelnost v pervoi gosudarstvennoi dume (St. Petersburg, 1907). An official party publication.

Pervaia burzhuazno-demokraticheskaia revoliutsiia v Rossii 1905–1907 gg., kratkii ukazatel literatury, A. M. Pankratova, ed. (Moscow, 1954). Soviet historiography since World War II.

Pervaia russkaia revoliutsiia, ukazatel literatury, G. K. Derman, ed. (Moscow, 1930).

Pervaia tsarskaia rech [by F. I. Rodichev] (Geneva, 1895).

Peshekhonov, A. V., "Avtobiografiia," in *Russkie vedomosti, 1863–1913* (listed separately), Part Two, pp. 142-146.

—— *Nakanune* (St. Petersburg, 1906).

—— *Na ocherednye temy* (St. Petersburg, 1904).

—— "Pochemu my togda ushli," *Russkoe bogatstvo* (St. Petersburg), November-December 1917. On 1906 split of Popular Socialists from the Socialist Revolutionary party.

———— "Voina i otechestvo," *Pravo* (St. Petersburg), 14 November 1904.

———— on Popular Socialist Party, in *Trud-Narod* (St. Petersburg), 1906, no. 1.

[Peshekhonov, A. V.], N. Novobrantsev (pseudonym), on liberalism and ideology of populism, *Revoliutsionnaia Rossiia* [Geneva], 15 September 1903 (no. 32) and 10 October 1903 (no. 33).

Petrunkevich, I. I., "Blizhaishie zadachi zemstva" (1879), in *Iubileinyi zemski sbornik* (listed separately).

———— *Iz zapisok obshchestvennogo deiatelia* (vol. XXI of *Arkhiv russkoi revoliutsii*, Berlin, 1934).

———— "Stranichka iz lichnykh vospominanii," in *Pamiati Goltseva* (listed separately). On the late 1870's.

———— "Voina i nashi zadachi," *Pravo* (St. Petersburg), 10 October 1904.

———— Letter to author on the late 1870's, in Bogucharski, *Iz istorii politicheskoi borby* (listed separately), pp. 397–404.

———— Preface to *Agrarnyi vopros* (listed separately).

P. N. Miliukov, 1859–1929, S. A. Smirov and others, ed. (Paris, [1929]). Contains bibliography.

Pogorelko, A. K., *Doklad kharkovskogo gorodskogo golovy o rezultatakh soveshchanii zemskikh i gorodskikh deiatelei [6-go noiabria 1904 g. — 14-go noiabria 1905 g.]* (Kharkov, 1905).

Politicheskii stroi sovremennykh gosudarstv, kn. P. D. Dolgorukov and I. I. Petrunkevich, ed. (St. Petersburg, 1905).

Polner, T. I., *Zhiznennyi put kniazia Georgiia Evg. Lvova* (Paris, 1932).

Postanovleniia oblastnogo sezda deiatelei po kustarnoi promyshlennosti v Poltave (Poltava, 1901).

Problemy idealizma, P. I. Novgorodtsev, ed. (St. Petersburg, 1902). Collective volume by former legal Marxists, including Berdiaev, Bulgakov, Struve [P.G.], Kistiakovski, and Frank.

Proekt osnovnogo zakona Rossiiskoi imperii, vyrabotan kommissiei biuro obshchezemskikh sezdov (vol. III of *Osvobozhdenie's Materialy po vyrabotke russkoi konstitutsii,* Paris, 1905).

Prokopovich, S. N., *K kritike Marksa* (St. Petersburg, 1901).

———— *Kooperativnoe dvizhenie v Rossii* (St. Petersburg, 1903).

———— *K rabochemu voprosu v Rossii* (St. Petersburg, 1905).

———— *Mestnye liudi o nuzhdakh Rossii* (St. Petersburg, 1904).

—— *Rabochee dvizhenie na zapade*, vol. I, *Germaniia, Belgiia* (St. Petersburg, 1899).

[Prokopovich, S. N.], *Martovskaia revoliutsiia v Germanii v 1848 godu* (Geneva, 1898).

—— N. N. (pseudonym), "Otvet na broshiuru Akselroda: 'K voprosu o sovremennykh zadachakh v taktike russkikh sotsial-demokratov'," in G. V. Plekhanov, *Sochineniia* (vol. XII, Moscow [1924]), pp. 500–516.

Protopopov, D. D., *Istoriia S.-Peterburgskogo komiteta gramotnosti sostoiavshego pri Imperatorskom volnom ekonomicheskom obshchestve, 1861–1895* (St. Petersburg, 1898).

Raeff, Marc, "The Peasant Commune in the Political Thinking of Russian Publicists, Laissez-faire Liberalism in the Reign of Alexander II" (Doctoral dissertation, Harvard University, 1950). Concentrating on eight leading "liberal conservatives," this new interpretation includes Koshelev and Chicherin.

Rodichev, F. I., "Avtobiografiia F. I. Rodicheva," *Vozrozhdenie* (Paris), 1954, no. 31. Autobiographical letter of 1932, touching on nationality question.

—— 'Dela minuvshikh dnei," *Rul* (Berlin), from 26 April 1927 to 29 April 1927 (nos. 1946–1949), four autobiographical installments on volunteering for Serbian war of 1876.

—— "Iz vospominanii," *Poslednie novosti* (Paris), irregular and nonchronological installments:
No. 3590 (20 January 1931), "Bakunin i nechaevshchina."
No. 3663 (3 April 1931), and no. 3664 (4 April 1931), "Posle 1 Marta 1881."
No. 3700 (10 May 1931), "Vybory v 1-iu gos. dumu."
No. 3832 (19 September 1931), "Obshchina i lichnost."
No. 3859 (16 October 1931), "Podatnye pokhody na krestian."
No. 4048 (22 April 1932), "O semeistve Bakuninykh i tverskom zemstve."
No. 4108 (21 June 1932), "Zemstvo i narodnoe obrazovanie."
No. 4533 (20 August 1933) (posthumous), "Detstvo."
No. 4790 (5 May 1934), "Vstrecha s Ogarevym."

—— "Iz vospominanii," *Sovremennye zapiski* (Paris), 1933, no. 53. On Tver address of 1895.

—— "The Liberal Movement in Russia (1855–1891)," *The Slavonic Review* (London), June 1923 (vol. II, no. 4).

[Rodichev, F. I.], *Pervaia tsarskaia rech* (listed separately).

Rozenberg, Vladimir, *Iz istorii russkoi pechati, organizatsiia obsh-*

chestvennogo mneniia v Rossii i nezavisimaia gazeta "Russkie vedomosti" (*1863–1918 gg.*) (Prague, 1924).

Rusanov, N. S., " 'Politika' N. K. Mikhailovskogo, iz vospominanii o nem i ego pisem," *Byloe* (St. Petersburg), July 1907.

Russian Thought and Politics, Hugh McLean, Martin E. Malia, and George Fischer, ed., vol. IV of Harvard Slavic Studies (Cambridge, 1957).

Russkaia mysl, monthly magazine (Moscow). See also Ulianov, *Ukazatel zhurnalnoi literatury.*

RUSSKIE VEDOMOSTI, daily newspaper (Moscow). *Russkie vedomosti, 1863–1913* (Moscow, 1913). Partly autobiographical "Who's Who" is in Part Two. See also Rozenberg, *Iz istorii.*

RUSSKOE BOGATSTVO, monthly magazine (St. Petersburg). *Ukazatel statei v zhurnale "Russkoe bogatstvo," 1893–1911 g.* (St. Petersburg, 1911). See also Ulianov, *Ukazatel zhurnalnoi literatury.*

Savelev, A., "Na zare osvoboditelnogo dvizheniia, vospominaniia starogo zemtsa o dvukh sezdakh, byvshikh v 1901 g., v Moskve s uchastiem zemskikh deiatelei," *Golos minuvshego* (Moscow), 1914, no. 1.

Samoderzhavie i zemstvo, konfidentsialnaia zapiska ministra finansov Stats-sekretaria S. Iu. Vitte, Petr Struve, ed. (Stuttgart, 1st ed., 1901, 2nd ed., 1903).

Schelting, Alexander von, *Russland und Europe im russischen Geschichtsdenken* (Bern, 1948). Early liberal thought.

Sef, S. E., *Burzhuaziia v 1905 godu, Po neizdannym arkhivnym materialam* (Moscow, 1926).

Sergei Andreevich Muromtsev, kn. D. I. Shakhovskoi, ed. (Moscow, 1911).

Shakhovskoi, kn. D. I., "Avtobiografiia," in *Russkie vedomosti, 1863–1913* (listed separately), Part Two, pp. 196–201.

———— "Politicheskie techeniia v russkom zemstve," in *Iubileinyi zemski sbornik* (listed separately).

———— "Soiuz osvobozhdeniia," *Zarnitsy* (St. Petersburg), 1909, no. 2, Part Two.

———— "V gody pereloma, otryvki vospominanii," *Vestnik selskogo khoziaistva* (Moscow), November-December 1920 (vol. XX, no. 4). Oppositional activity in 1895, 1901, and 1905, including the Moscow Agricultural Society.

[Shakhovskoi, kn. D. I.], *Adresa zemstv* (listed under Mirnyi).

Shipov, D. N., *K voprosu o vzaimnykh otnosheniiakh gubernskikh i uezdnykh zemstv* (Moscow, 1899).

—— *Vospominaniia i dumy o perezhitom* (Moscow, 1918).

[Shipov, D. N., and others], *K mneniiu menshinstva chastnogo soveshchaniia zemskikh deiatelei [noiabria 1904 g.]* (Moscow, 1905).

Shreider, G. I., "Avtobiografiia," in *Russkie vedomosti, 1863–1913* (listed separately), Part Two, pp. 203–205.

—— *Nashe gorodskoe obshchestvennoe upravlenie* (vol. I, St. Petersburg, 1905).

Skalon, V. Iu., *Zemskie voprosy, ocherki i obozreniia* (Moscow, 1882).

—— *Zemskie vzgliady na reformu mestnogo upravleniia, obzor zemskikh otzyvov i proektov* (Moscow, 1884).

[Skalon, V. Iu.], *Mneniia zemskikh sobranii o sovremennom polozhenii Rossii* (Berlin, 1883).

S.-Peterburgskie vedomosti, daily newspaper (St. Petersburg). See also Korsh, *Etiudy*.

Sputnik izbiratelia na 1906 god (St. Petersburg [1906]).

M. M. Stasiulevich i ego sovremenniki v ikh perepiske, ed. M. K. Lemke (5 vols., St. Petersburg, 1911–1913).

Struve, P. B., "M. V. Chelnokov i D. N. Shipov, glava iz moikh vospominanii," *Novyi zhurnal* (New York), 1949, no. 22.

—— *Kriticheskie zametki k voprosu ob ekonomicheskom razvitii Rossii* (St. Petersburg, 1894).

—— *Marksovaia teoriia sotsialnogo razvitiia* (Kiev, 1905). First published as "Die Marxsche Theorie der sozialen Entwicklung," *Archiv für Soziale Gesetzgebung und Statistik* (Berlin), 1899, vol. 14, no. 5–6.

—— "My Contacts and Conflicts with Lenin," *The Slavonic and East European Review* (London), Part One, April 1934 (vol. XII, no. 36) and Part Two, July 1934 (vol. XIII, no. 37).

—— "My Contacts with Rodichev," *The Slavonic and East European Review* (London), January 1934 (vol. XII, no. 35).

—— *Na raznye temy (1893–1903 gg.)* (St. Petersburg, 1902).

—— "Samoderzhavie i zemstvo," *Iskra* (Munich), February 1901 (no. 2) and May 1901 (no. 4).

—— *Sotsialnaia i ekonomicheskaia istoriia Rossii* (Paris, 1952), 350–380. Contains bibliography.

—— Preface to Berdiaev, *Subektivism i individualizm v obshchestvennoi filosofii* (listed separately).

—— Preface to *Loi fondamentale de l'Empire Russe* (listed separately). Comments on constitutional and nationality questions. See also biographical studies by Frank and Nicolaevsky. Almost each issue of *Osvobozhdenie* and of the *Osvobozhdenie* pamphlet series contains at least one item by Struve.

[Struve, P. B.] P. Inorodzew (pseudonym), "Die Arbeiterbewegung in Russland," *Soziale Praxis, Zentralblatt für Sozialpolitik* (Berlin), 8 October 1896.

—— Peterburzhets (pseudonym), "Po povodu peterburgskoi stachki," *Rabotnik* (Geneva), 1897, no. 3–4.

—— R. N. S. (pseudonym), Preface to first edition of *Samoderzhavie i zemstvo* (listed separately).

—— P. G. (pseudonym), *Problemy idealizma* (listed separately).

—— Agricultural report of Russian Social Democrats at London congress of Socialist International (1896), in G. V. Plekhanov, *Sochineniia* (vol. IX, Moscow [1923]), pp. 352–367.

[Takhtarev, K. M.] Peterburzhets (pseudonym), *Ocherk Peterburzhskogo rabochego dvizheniia 90-kh godov, po lichnym vospominaniiam* (London, 1902).

Trubetskaia, kniazhna Olga, *Kniaz S. N. Trubetskoi, vospominaniia sestry* (New York, 1953). Trubetskoi writings appended.

Trubetskoi, kn. E. N., *Vospominaniia* (Sofia, 1921).

Trubetskoi, kn. S. N., *Sobranie sochinenii* (Moscow, vol. I, 1907, vol. II, 1908).

See also Trubetskaia, *Kniaz S. N. Trubetskoi*.

"Trudovaia (narodno-sotsialisticheskaia) partiia, programma i skhema organizatsii," Supplement to *Narodno-sotsialisticheskoe obozrenie* (St. Petersburg), 1906, no. 1.

Trudy kommissii po voprosam zemskoi statistiki [Imperatorskogo volnogo ekonomicheskogo obshchestva], zasedaniia statisticheskoi kommissii s 15 po 22 fevralia 1901 g. (St. Petersburg, 1901).

Trudy podsektsii statistiki XI sezda russkikh estestvoispytatelei i vrachei v S.-Peterburge 20–30 dekabria 1901 g. (St. Petersburg, 1902).

Trudy sezda deiatelei agronomicheskoi pomoshchi mestnomu naseleniiu (Moscow, 1901).

Trudy vserossiiskogo sezda selskikh khoziaev sozvannogo Imperatorskim moskovskim obshchestvom selskogo khoziaistva s 10 po 20 dekabria 1895 g. (vol. I, Moscow, 1897). This volume describes origins and decisions of conference.

Tugan-Baranovski, M., *Ocherki po noveishei istorii politicheskoi ekonomii* (St. Petersburg, 1903).

——— *Promyshlennye krizisy v sovremennoi Anglii* (St. Petersburg, 1894).

——— *Russkaia fabrika v proshlom i v nastoiashchem* (St. Petersburg, 1908).

——— *Teoreticheskie osnovy marksizma* (St. Petersburg, 1905).

TVER. G. A. Dzhanshiev, "Rol tverskogo zemstva v krestianskoi reforme," in his *Epokha velikikh reform* (10th ed., St. Petersburg, 1908).
Sbornik materialov dlia istorii tverskogo gubernskogo zemstva, 1866–1882 g., P. A. Korsakov, ed. (6 vols., Tver, 1884).
Zemskie deiateli tverskoi gubernii (vol. I, Tver, 1909).
See also Dzhanshiev, *Unkovski;* "Epizod iz istorii obshchestvennykh dvizhenii," in *Osvobozhdenie,* Book One; Kornilov, *Semeistvo Bakuninykh;* Rodichev, "Iz vospominanii," in *Poslednie novosti* and *Sovremennye zapiski;* and Veselovski, *Istoricheskii ocherk.*

Tyrkova-Williams, A., *Na putiakh k svobode* (New York, 1952).

——— *To, chego bolshe ne budet* (Paris [1954]).

Ulianov, N. A., *Ukazatel zhurnalnoi literatury* (vol. II, Moscow, 1913). This volume covers 1896–1905. It includes the liberal *Vestnik Evropy,* the liberal-populist *Russkaia mysl,* the populist *Russkoe bogatstvo,* and the legal Marxist *Nachalo, Novoe slovo, Zhizn,* and *Mir bozhii.*

UNION OF LIBERATION [Soiuz osvobozhdeniia], *Bolshaia sovetskaia entsiklopediia* (1st ed., vol. 52, Moscow, 1947), p. 342.
Kakovy nashi poriadki i chto nuzhno dlia uluchsheniia narodnoi zhizni ([Paris], 1905). Pamphlet printed by the Union of Liberation in mid-1905 for mass distribution.

Union of Liberation, *Listok Soiuza osvobozhdeniia.* Six one-page issues published in St. Petersburg clandestinely during 1905: 15 May, 28 May, 8 June, 20 June, 27 June, 4 September.

——— 1904 program, *Listok Osvobozhdeniia* no. 17, 19 November, 1904.

——— 1905 program, *Osvobozhdenie* no. 69–70, 7 May 1905.
See also essays by Shakhovskoi and Vodovozov.

Vekhi, sbornik statei o russkoi intelligentsii, M. Gershenzon, ed. (Moscow, 1909). Fourth edition, 1910, contains bibliography on *Vekhi* controversy. Except for the editor, the contributors are the same ones who in 1902 published *Problemy idealizma* (listed separately).

Veselovski, B. B., *Istoriia zemstva za sorok let* (St. Petersburg, vol. I and vol. II, 1909, vol. III and vol. IV, 1911). Detailed bibliography in first and last volume. *Istoriia zemstva* is analyzed in review article by Kornilov (listed separately).

—— *Istoricheskii ocherk deiatelnosti zemskikh uchrezhdenii Tverskoi gubernii, 1864–1913 gg.* (Tver, 1914).

—— coeditor, *Iubileinyi zemskii sbornik* (listed separately).

VESTNIK EVROPY, monthly magazine (St. Petersburg).
Katalog zhurnala Vestnik Evropy za 25 let, 1866–1890 (St. Petersburg, 1890).
See also *Stasiulevich i ego sovremenniki*, and Ulianov, *Ukazatel zhurnalnoi literatury*.

Vinaver, M. M., *Nedavnee* (3rd ed., Paris, 1926).

[Vodovozov, V. V.], "Osvobozhdeniia Soiuz," *Slovar Brokgauz-Efron* (supplementary vol. II, St. Petersburg, 1906), p. 354. See also note, p. 142, on Vodovozov's unpublished history of the Union of Liberation.

Weber, Max, "Russlands Übergang zum Scheinkonstitutionalismus," *Archiv für Sozialwissenschaft und Sozialpolitik* (Tübingen), 1906, vol. XXIII. On the political institutions growing out of the 1905 revolution.

—— "Zur Lage der bürgerlichen Demokratie in Russland," *Archiv für Sozialwissenschaft und Sozialpolitik* (Tübingen), 1906, vol. XXII. Russian liberalism analyzed through the "Union of Liberation constitution" of 1904.

Witte, S. Iu., *Samoderzhavie i zemstvo* (listed under title).

Zander, L. A., *Bog i mir, mirosozertsanie o. S. Bulgakova* (2 vols., Paris, 1948). Volume II contains Bulgakov bibliography.

Koshelev

Skalon

Muromtsev

Arsenev

Shipov

GENTRY LEADERS IN 1905

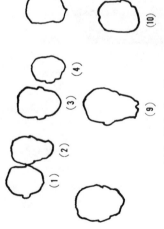

(1) Nikolai Lvov
(2) Rodichev
(3) Georgi Lvov
(4) Golovin
(5) Pavel Dolgorukov

(6) Sergei Trubetskoi
(7) Novosiltsev
(8) Shakhovskoi
(9) Geiden
(10) Petrunkevich

INTELLIGENTSIA LEADERS

Dragomanov

Annenski

Struve

Miliukov

Prokopovich

Notes

Chapter One. Small Deeds or Senseless Dreams?

1. Statistics in Veselovski, *Istoriia zemstva*, III, 47–50.
2. Aleksandr Potresov in *Obshchestvennoe dvizhenie v Rossii*, I, 642.
3. English text in Miliukov, *Russia and its Crisis*, 280.
4. S.-*Peterburgskie vedomosti* (1866), no. 342.
5. Text in Chicherin, *Vospominaniia*, IV, 169–174.
6. Koshelev, *Zapiski*, 76–78 and 249–251.
7. Koshelev, *Konstitutsia, samoderzhavie, i zemskaia duma*, 36–40, 47.
8. Photographs in Belokonski, *Zemskoe dvizhenie*, 57, 388. See also photograph in this book.
9. Text in Shipov, *Vospominaniia i dumy o perezhitom*, 150–152.
10. [Shipov and others], *K mneniiu menshinstva chastnogo zasedaniia zemskikh deiatelei*, 7–8.
11. Shipov, *Vospominaniia i dumy o perezhitom*, 269–270.
12. Shipov, *Vospominaniia i dumy o perezhitom*, 271.
13. Text of speech in Shipov, *Vospominaniia i dumy o perezhitom*, 81–84.
14. Text in *Osvobozhdenie*, Book I, 19–20.
15. List of provinces in Oganovski, *Selskoe khoziaistvo Rossii v XX veke*, 6–9.
16. Petrunkevich in *Pamiati Goltseva*, 106, and Petrunkevich, *Iz zapisok obshchestvennogo deiatelia*, 15, 112.
17. Photographs in Petrunkevich, *Iz zapisok obshchestvennogo deiatelia*, [3], and Belokonski, *Zemskoe dvizhenie*, 289. See also photograph in this book.
18. Debogori-Mokrievich, *Vospominaniia*, I, 300.
19. Text in Burtsev, *Za sto let*, Part One, 143–146.
20. Petrunkevich in *Iubileinyi zemskii sbornik*, 432, and Petrunkevich, *Iz zapisok obshchestvennogo deiatelia*, 110.
21. Text of pamphlet in *Iubileinyi zemskii sbornik*, 429–436. This version has a blank instead of the concluding two words, which are taken from Petrunkevich, *Iz zapisok obshchestvennogo deiatelia*, 456.

22. Petrunkevich in *Pamiati Goltseva*, 109.
23. Text of program in Burtsev, *Za sto let*, Part One, 209–211.
24. *Vestnik Evropy*, March 1881, 340.

Chapter Two. Sons and Grandsons

1. *Doklad komissii Moskovskogo universiteta*, 59.
2. Statistics in *Doklad komissii Moskovskogo universiteta*, 1–2.
3. *Izvlecheniia iz knigi A. I. Georgievskogo* 1.
4. Maklakov, *Iz vospominanii*, 61, 62.
5. Not untypical are the 1897 proceedings of an outspoken and heterodox debate on the influence of harvests and bread prices on economic life: [Chuprov and others], *Vliianie urozhaev i khlebnykh tsen na raznye storony ekonomicheskoi zhizni, doklad prof. A. I. Chuprova i preniia v III otdelenii Imperatorskogo volnogo ekonomicheskogo obshchestva.*
6. The revealing correspondence in this long and stubborn contest was published by the Economic Society in 1904: "Iz del komissii po peresmotru ustava I.v.e. obshchestva v 1900 g."
7. Membership list as of 1 January 1900, in Imperial Free Economic Society, *Otchet o deistviiakh za 1899 god*, 123–147.
8. Statistic in Protopopov, *Istoriia S.-Peterburgskogo komiteta gramotnosti*, xiv–xix.
9. Statistic in Veselovski, *Istoriia zemstva*, III, 494.
10. List in Veselovski, *Istoriia zemstva*, III, 467. An example of the gentry entering the third element is Prince Vladimir Obolenski, long a zemstvo statistician.
11. Quoted by Miliukov, "Biograficheskii ocherk," in *Sergei Aleksandrovich Muromtsev*, 30.
12. Muromtsev, *Stati i rechi*, III, 1–128.
13. Muromtsev, *Stati i rechi*, V, 1.
14. Authors identified in Muromtsev, *Stati i rechi*, V, 11.
15. English translation in Kennan, "The Last Appeal of Russian Liberals," 56–63. Originally published abroad as pamphlet: [Muromtsev and others], *V pervye dni ministerstva gr. M. T. Loris–Melikova.*
16. Miliukov, Jubilee edition of *Ocherki po istorii russkoi kultury*, I, 5.
17. Miliukov, *Ocherki po istorii russkoi kultury*, I, 18. Miliukov's views were also expounded in his seven little known annual surveys of Russian literature for a staid London journal, the *Athenaeum*, between 1889 and 1896.
18. Miliukov, *Iz istorii russkoi intelligentsii*, 267.

19. Text in *Russkii vestnik*, November 1887, 273–282.
20. English translation in Struve, "My Contacts with Rodichev," 349–350.
21. English translation in Struve, "My Contacts with Rodichev," 350.
22. *Pervaia tsarskaia rech.*
23. S. Mirnyi, *Adresa zemstv.*
24. Text in *Trudy Vserossiiskogo sezda selskikh khoziaev*, I, 39–63.
25. Shakhovskoi, "V gody pereloma," 25–26.
26. Text of correspondence in Shipov, *Vospominaniia i dumy o perezhitom*, 63–65.
27. Text of correspondence in Shipov, *Vospominaniia i dumy o perezhitom*, 76–80.
28. Text in Shipov, *Vospominaniia i dumy o perezhitom*, 81–85.

Chapter Three. Third Force

1. *Vestnik Evropy*, October 1895, 788.
2. Text in Burtsev, *Za sto let*, Part One, 148–152.
3. Petrunkevich, *Iz zapisok obshchestvennogo deiatelia*, 195.
4. Korolenko, *Pisma*, 20, 29, 302–305.
5. Gorki, *Sobranie sochinenii*, 2d ed., XXII, 130.
6. Text in Burtsev, *Za sto let*, Part One, 26–262.
7. Korolenko, *Pisma*, 303–304. Emphasis by Korolenko.
8. Rusanov, " 'Politika' Mikhailovskogo," 135.
9. Peshekhonov, "Pochemu my togda ushli," 329.
10. Berdiaev, *Samopoznanie*, 14, 144.
11. Martov, *Zapiski sotsialdemokrata*, 91.
12. Struve, "My Contacts with Rodichev," 351.
13. Text in Struve, "My Contacts with Rodichev," 352–354.
14. Struve, "My Contacts and Conflicts with Lenin," Part One, 575–580. Emphasis by Struve.
15. Struve, *Na raznye temy*, 300.
16. Struve, *Kriticheskie zametki*, ix, 46, 130.
17. *Materialy k kharakteristike nashego khoziastvennogo razvitiia.*
18. Text in Plekhanov, *Sochineniia*, IX, 352–367.
19. Peterburzhets, "Po povodu peterburgskoi stachki," xv–xvi (emphasis by Struve), and P. Inorodzew, "Die Arbeiterbewegung in Russland."
20. Struve, "My Contacts and Conflicts with Lenin," Part Two, 75.
21. Text in Lenin, *Sochineniia*, 3rd ed., II, 615–617.
22. Struve, *Na raznye temy*, ii.
23. Partial text in *Obshchestvennoe dvizhenie v Rossii*, I, 615–616.

24. *Samoderzhavie i zemstvo* was the title of both pamphlet and article.

25. Lenin, "Goniteli zemstva i annibaly liberalizma." Correspondence appears in third volume of *Leninskii sbornik*.

26. Struve, *Na raznye temy*, 301.

27. Partial text of Struve letter in *Sotsial–demokraticheskoe dvizhenie v Rossii*, 348.

28. Prokopovich, *Rabochee dvizhenie na zapade*, I, i.

29. During this interim period, the orthodox Union of Russian Social Democrats in Geneva published three pamphlets by the future theoretical economists: *Stachka lzhi and Son pod 1-oe maia* by Kuskova, and *Martovskaia revoliutsiia v Germanii* by Prokopovich.

30. Text of programmatic statements by practical economists in [Takhtarev], *Ocherk peterburzhskogo rabochego dvizheniia*, 81–85, and Lenin, *Sochineniia*, 3rd ed., II, 611–612.

31. Prokopovich in Plekhanov, *Sochineniia*, XII, 509.

32. Kuskova in Plekhanov, *Sochineniia*, XII, 493.

33. Prokopovich, *K kritike Marksa*, 248.

34. Prokopovich, in Plekhanov *Sochineniia*, XII, 514.

35. Bernstein, *Die Voraussetzungen des Sozialismus und die Aufgaben der Sozialdemokratie*, 173–174, footnote.

36. English translation in Lenin, *Selected Works*, I, 516–520.

37. Berdiaev, *Sub specie aeternitatis*, 382.

Chapter Four. From Right to Left

1. The earliest Symposium publication was the only one to appear abroad: A.P., *Samoderzhavie, biurokratizm i zemstvo*. The others, published in Russia jointly with the liberal legal journal *Pravo*, were *Melkaia zemskaia edinitsa, Nuzhdy derevni, Krestianskii stroi, Agrarnyi vopros, Politicheskii stroi sovremennykh gosudarstv*.

2. List of leading participants in Veselovski, *Istoriia zemstva*, III, 554.

3. Text in Lenin, *Sochineniia*, 3rd ed., V, 74–78.

4. List of participants in Shipov, *Vospominaniia i dumy o perezhitom*, 160–161.

5. Text of the minutes in Struve preface to Witte, *Samoderzhavie i zemstvo*, 1903 edition, lviii–lxviii.

6. Text of platform in *Osvobozhdenie*, no. 5, 19 August 1905, 65–66.

7. Text of government reprimand in *Osvobozhdenie* no. 6, 2 September 1902, 82.

8. Text of replies in *Osvobozhdenie*, no. 10, 2 November 1902,

146–147, and *Osvobozhdenie*, no. 11, 18 November 1902, 176–177.

9. Minutes of interviews in Shipov, *Vospominaniia i dumy o perezhitom*, 171–184.

10. *Osvobozhdenie*, no. 15, 19 January 1903, 250.

11. Text of resolution, and list of leading participants, in *Osvobozhdenie*, no. 23, 19 May 1903, 420.

12. List of participants in Shipov, *Vospominaniia i dumy o perezhitom*, 219–220.

13. Text in Belokonski, *Zemskoe dvizhenie*, 163.

14. List in Veselovski, *Istoriia zemstva*, III, 577, footnote.

15. List in Petrunkevich, *Iz zapisok obshchestvennogo deiatelia*, 338.

16. Shakhovskoi, "Souiz osvobozhdeniia," 106. This discussion was subsequently reflected by the participant Bulgakov: L., "K agrarnomu voprosu," *Osvobozhdenie*, no. 33, 19 October 1903.

17. Minutes of fourth and last congress of the Group of Zemstvo Constitutionalists (July 1905) in *Osvobozhdenie*, no. 78–79, 5 October 1905, Supplement, 1–14.

18. List in Shakhovskoi, "Souiz osvobozhdeniia," 110.

19. Shakhovskoi, "Souiz osvobozhdeniia," 111.

20. Text first made public in *Listok Osvobozhdeniia*, no. 17, 19 November 1904, 2.

21. Text in "Liberalnaia partiia i vneshniaia politika Rossii," *Osvobozhdenie*, no. 33, 19 February 1904.

22. Partial text in Pg., "Politika liberalnoi partii," *Osvobozhdenie*, no. 44, 19 March 1904.

23. List in "Soiuz osvobozhdeniia," *Bolshaia sovetskaia entsiklopedia*, 1st ed., vol. 52, 342.

Chapter Five. Prologue to Revolution

1. *Listok Osvobozhdeniia*, no. 1, 24 February 1904.

2. *Osvobozhdenie*, no. 43, 7 March 1904.

3. *Pravo*, 10 October 1904.

4. *Pravo*, 14 November 1904.

5. Text in Shakhovskoi, "Soiuz osvobozhdeniia," 120–121. Emphasis in original.

6. Text in *Osvobozhdenie*, no. 57, 15 October 1904. Miliukov's article appeared in *Osvobozhdenie*, no. 52, 19 July 1904.

7. Text of minutes of meetings of Social Democratic central committee accepting and then rejecting Paris Conference invitation in *Sotsialdemokraticheskoe dvizhenie v Rossii*, 325–337, and Volkovicher, "Partiia i russko-iaponskaia voina," 119–120.

8. Text of police report on Paris conference in "Doklad Rataeva."

9. *Revoliutsionnaia Rossiia*, no. 74, 1 September 1905, 27–28, and Zilliacus, *Revolution und Gegenrevolution*, 88–89.

10. Text in *Revoliutsionnaia Rossiia*, no. 56, 5 December 1904, 1–2.

11. Text in *Listok Osvobozhdeniia*, no. 17, 19 November 1904, 1–2. English translation of quoted passage in Miliukov, *Russia and its Crisis*, 524–525.

12. [Vodovozov], "Osvobozhdeniia Soiuz," 354.

13. *Osnovnoi gosudarstvennyi zakon*, 58-59.

14. *Osnovnoi gosudarstvennyi zakon*, 33–34.

15. Text in *Osvobozhdeniie*, no. 69–70, 7 May 1905, 305–8ᴄᴄ.

16. Kokoshkin in *Sergei Aleksandrovich Muromtsev*, 222.

17. Text in *Proekt osnovnogo zakona Rossiiskoi imperii*.

18. Text in [Bogucharski], Editorial Note in *Istoricheskii sbornik "Nasha strana,"* 29, footnote.

19. Shipov, *Vospominaniia i dumy o perezhitom*, 241.

20. List in *Chastnoe soveshchanie zemskikh deiatelei*, 1–8.

21. Text and bureau's Explanatory Note in *Chastnoe soveshchanie zemskikh deiatelei*, 132–141.

22. Text of Petrunkevich and Briukhatov speeches, *Chastnoe soveschanie zemskikh deiatelei*, 52–56.

23. Text of Shipov speech in *Chastnoe soveschanie zemskikh deiatelei*, 58–61. An outgrowth of this debate was the separate pamphlet, [Shipov and others], *K mneniu menshinstva chastnogo zasedaniia zemskikh deiatelei*.

24. Text of Lvov, Kokoshkin and Petrunkevich speeches in *Chastnoe soveshchanie zemskikh deiatelei*, 78–85.

25. Text in *Chastnoe soveshchanie zemskikh deiatelei*, 141–145. A comparative text of final and draft resolutions appears in Shipov, *Vospominaniia i dumy o perezhitom*, 261–265.

26. Text in Trubetskaia, *Kniaz S.N. Trubetskoi*, 138-141.

27. Text in Shipov, *Vospominaniia i dumy o perezhitom*, 581–587.

28. Text of resolutions in *Chastnoe soveshchanie zemskikh deiatelei*, 150–223.

29. Text of resolutions in Belokonski, *Zemskoe dvizhenie*, 276–281, 286–287, 330–332, 364–388.

30. Text of resolutions in *Chastnoe soveshchanie gorodskikh deiatelei*.

31. Text of resolutions in Supplement of Sef, *Burzhuaziia v 1905 godu*.

32. Text of *Listok Osvobozhdeniia*, no. 21, 9 December 1904, 3.

33. Miliukov, *Russia and its Crisis*, 530.

34. English translation in *Introduction to Contemporary Civilization in the West* (1st ed.), II, 755–758. Gapon's contacts with the Union of Liberation are mentioned in his own *Istoriia moei zhizni*, by [Bogucharski] in Editorial Note in *Istoricheskii Sbornik "Nasha strana,"* 30, footnote, and in several reminiscences by Gapon's worker associates enumerated in [Nevski], "Bibliografiia o zubatovskikh soiuzakh."

35. The program of this and most other post-1905 parties, together with a comparative table of the programs, appears in *Sputnik izbiratelia na 1906 god*, 168–233. The program of the Party of Peaceful Regeneration is in *Partiia mirnogo obnovleniia, ee obrazovanie i deiatelnost*, 185–188, while that of another splinter group between Kadets and Octobrists — the Party of Democratic Reforms of older moderate constitutionalists like Arsenev and Stasiulevich — is part of the *Sputnik izbiratelia* already cited. The founders' statement, "Trudovaia (Narodno-sotsialisticheskaia) partiia," includes the Popular Socialist program.

INDEX

Russian Research Center Studies

* Out of print.
† Publications of the Harvard Project on the Soviet Social System.
‡ Published jointly with the Center for International Affairs, Harvard University.